Problems of Language
and Learning

Problems of Language and Learning

Edited by
ALAN DAVIES

HEINEMANN
LONDON
in association with the
SSRC and SsRE

Heinemann Educational Books Ltd
LONDON EDINBURGH MELBOURNE AUCKLAND TORONTO
SINGAPORE HONG KONG KUALA LUMPUR
IBADAN NAIROBI JOHANNESBURG
LUSAKA NEW DELHI

ISBN 0 435 10190 0

Set in Baskerville

Published by
Heinemann Educational Books Ltd
48 Charles Street, London W1X 8AH
Printed in Great Britain by
Butler & Tanner Ltd., Frome and London

Contents

Foreword

The papers in this book were prepared for a seminar organised by a committee chaired by Dr. W. B. Dockrell and sponsored by the Educational Research Board of the Social Science Research Council. The Board is currently arranging several of these seminars in areas of research where there is a particularly rapid development of ideas which are thought likely to influence the future pattern of educational thinking. The topic of language and learning was an obvious choice for such a seminar. Other topics which seminars have so far covered are computers in education, teacher education and classroom observation. The seminars have a dual purpose; to promote the exchange of information and discussion of new methodologies among research workers in these areas of inquiry; and to provide a stimulus to new and promising directions of research.

Inevitably, the size of a seminar group must be limited. But the discussion among the relatively small group of participants is of interest and value to a wider public—not only other research workers and students but also teachers and administrators—who have much to gain from eavesdropping on the debate. For them, this record of the seminar provides an up-to-date review of important issues. If it succeeds also in sharpening thinking and helping understanding of current trends of research on language and learning, the seminar will have fully achieved its purpose.

JOHN NISBET
Professor of Education, Aberdeen University; Chairman SSRC Educational Research Board

JEREMY MITCHELL
Secretary, Social Science Research Council

Introduction

1 *Aims and Successes*

This volume reports on the Seminar on Language and Learning which was run by the Scottish Council for Research in Education in January 1973 and which was sponsored by the SSRC.

From the beginning the Seminar was conceived as the first of two parts. This original intention remained, and the second Seminar took place in January 1974. The 1973 Seminar was intended to provide a clearing of the ground which would, if possible, do three things. First, it would provide the theoretical background to the relationship between language and learning so that the second (1974) Seminar could concentrate on the practical aspect. Second, it should try to reveal one or more research areas which the 1974 Seminar could deal with in depth. Third, it might throw up a number of suggestions of practical applications which could be seized on by interested groups and individuals and tested both by more formal research methods and by informal 'exploration' (see below) by teachers working with their own pupils.

The 1973 Seminar had some success in all three of these areas. As to the first (providing the theoretical background) the more theoretical parts of the discussion made clear the difficulties that exist in inter-disciplinary communication, even when the various disciplines are trying to focus on the same problem. Not only do they use different approaches and metalanguages but they do not even agree as to what is 'the problem'. Our Chairman reminded us several times how disciplines create problems so that what counts as a problem in, say, the psychology of language is not seen as a problem in sociolinguistics. Again, the papers and discussions in this Seminar stressed how little theory there yet is concerning total human behaviour, and a strong need was expressed for more work in fundamental linguistic theory which could have a bearing on language in use.

This could have satisfied the second aim of the Seminar (reveal a research area). Had they been asked to express a preference for the most important research area to work in over the next period several participants would have opted for research in theoretical linguistics as related to language in use. However, this could not be selected as the topic for the 1974 Seminar. The time was too short between the two Seminars to achieve anything in such work, and in any case the majority feeling in the 1973 Seminar was that the 1974 Seminar ought to concentrate on practical isssues. Even if we were short on theory the need was there for application research; and in any case there were practical pedagogic considerations that weighed as heavily in the area of language and learning as theoretical linguistic ones. With the practical issues in mind, the 1974 Seminar was to concentrate on reports from research projects dealing with young children's language. It was hoped that in these research projects a need for a joint approach to language and learning would be demonstrated. An argument for this was given in the Chairman's concluding summary when he suggested that the psychological and sociological approaches to language, which had kept prominently apart during the 1973 Seminar, needed to come together. He indicated that since the psychological approach is concerned with acquisition and the sociological with transmission they could conveniently meet in a 'Transmission–Acquisition Matrix'.

In relation to the third aim (suggestions of practical applications) a number of fairly specific points for research and exploration came up in the Seminar. They were:

children's spoken language as an interaction between teacher and child;

children's reading, and adults' image of it in terms of what is regarded as success;

adults' categorising of children's writing and its relationship to the children's own categorising and to formal linguistic indications of such categories;

formal and informal descriptions of varieties of spoken and written texts and their consideration of what sociological assumptions we make in assigning texts to one variety rather than another;

the need for teachers and pupils to engage in exploration of language in use, that is to say, collecting, examining and enjoying together the language data that surrounds us all.

2 *Plan of Seminar*

The time-table of the Seminar was as follows:

Session	Subject	Speaker	Discussant
DAY 1			
1	Sociolinguistics	M. A. K. Halliday	C. Criper
2	Dialect	H. H. Speitel	Gill Brown
3	Psychology	J. S. Bruner	C. Fraser
DAY 2			
4	Teaching of Reading	Margaret Clark	J. Merritt
5	Teaching of Writing	J. Britton	W. Gatherer
6	Summary, Chairman's Remarks	B. Bernstein	

Basil Bernstein chaired the proceedings of all the sessions. The main papers (see List of Contents for the exact titles) had been circulated beforehand. Each author briefly introduced his paper, and was followed by the discussant who read a prepared statement commenting on the paper. The discussants' remarks had not been previously circulated. Then followed open discussion among the thirty-odd participants. The whole proceedings were tape-recorded and a transcript made afterwards of selected parts of the discussions.

Presented in this volume are the original papers, revised versions of the discussants' remarks and an edited version of the transcribed selections mentioned above. The bibliographies have been collated and an index provided, as well as a list of participants.

3 *Main Concerns*

I want now to summarise what seemed to me the general outcome of the Seminar. I shall then discuss some of the more particular outcomes of each session.

The Seminar came back time and time again to five concerns. The fact that this happened suggests that the original concept of the Seminar did have some unity. The *first* of these concerns was the sheer difficulty of trying to bring a multi-disciplinary approach to bear on language and learning. Of course it is well known that such approaches are difficult, hence the Seminar. The difficulty exists at every level: the vocabulary is different, the categorising different, the explanations for the 'same' problem are different, and the 'problem' itself assumes a different form for each discipline.

The *second* concern was that in all our attempts to focus on practical problems we were constantly being hindered by our lack of theoretical knowledge. Again and again we found it impossible to formulate the problem and devise a methodology for analysis and description because we lacked the supporting theory. In his final summary the Chairman stressed the need for work in theoretical linguistics, though it was clear that this had to be linguistics in relation to language in use, since, as he reminded us, there are many different kinds of linguistics.

The *third* concern of the Seminar which developed from the previous one was the need for more adequate linguistic descriptions of language in use. For these to be made, more general categories are needed; *ad hoc* categories are fine for the 'exploration' type of work noted above but are of little use for advancing research. Here again, then, stemming from a lack of linguistic descriptions was a plea for better theory, which others could then use in their study of learning problems.

The *fourth* concern was with dialect. It was clear from Speitel's paper that dialect interference as a linguistic hindrance to intelligibility in Scotland would not be a crucial issue at the Seminar. What is really significant about dialect in Scotland is not whether it creates intelligibility problems but what attitudes people have towards it. Whether or not a pupil in a Scottish school understands his teacher depends to a large extent on whether he is prepared to accept his teacher's speech as belonging to a non-hostile dialect. What Labov has established empirically in New York seems to make sense in Scotland in the light of the experiences related by members of the Seminar.

The *fifth* concern takes us back to the first. If inter-disciplinary cooperation is so intrinsically difficult then perhaps a new discipline or sub-discipline is needed, free to develop its own language and delineate its own problems. This seemed to be what the Chairman meant when he called for work not in sociolinguistics on transmission only, nor in psychology on acquisition only, but in both together, within what he called the Transmission–Acquisition Matrix. The difficulties in the way of such an approach are formidable but the 1974 Seminar was to have more to say on it. Bernstein's formulation brought us back to an earlier remark by Halliday who had said that he assumed he had always been doing linguistics but that others now used the term sociolinguistics for what he understood to be linguistics.

A crucial stage in a child's learning comes when he enters primary school and fortunately there was an opportunity in the 1974 Seminar to examine the demands of this cross-over stage (from baby to school-child), affecting, as it does, acquisition and transmission, both in an institutional context.

4. Points of Detail

Particular points that emerged from the Seminar, session by session, were as follows:

Session 1 Short as we are on theory for language in use, Halliday tried to provide us with an overall view of the social conditions of language use. But we were reminded that however much language and society come together they are not the same, so that it is possible, and Criper made this point strongly, to overdo the correspondence by making the assumption of complete reflexion between language and society. Halliday wanted to reintroduce the term Register (or Language Variety) at this point as a kind of intermediate level 'between the linguistic system on the one hand and Bernstein's codes on the other' (p. 31).

Session 2 The Seminar accepted Speitel's case for a definable Standard Scottish English. Since this is definable in terms of cited forms only, the whole area of the relationship between teacher and pupil in terms of their normal pronunciation and the attitudes it evokes is open to investigation.

Lurking in the background of this Seminar all the time was the question about the normative influence of the school on dialects. Granted the existence of dialect, the critical question is just how far the child is free to use his dialect in school, in the same way as in more casual situations, e.g. the bus or the shop. In other words, how special a situation is the school? Whether or not it is 'special' in its linguistic influence, school is certainly a critical situation if only because of the amount of time children spend there.

Session 3 It was interesting here to see the proposal of *analytic competence* as the mature fusion of language and thought, thus joining the strictly linguistic competence and the more socio-linguistic communicative competence. Bruner posited analytic competence as the third stage when language and thought come together. Fraser wanted to make it clear that the social psychologist and the cognitive psychologist have different approaches, underlining again the difficulty of inter-disciplinary communication. Bernstein underlined this communication difficulty further when he denied the validity of Bruner's general 'universalist' approach, and stressed the importance of particular contexts.

Session 4 Margaret Clark's admonition to focus on success in reading and to specify objectively what is available to the successful reader, and what he has to aim at in terms of adult reading behaviour, was well taken. At the same time there was the realisation that success is sometimes illuminated by failures (as e.g. in error analysis studies in applied linguistics), and that specifying objectives may involve constructing tasks that become tests which of their nature capitalise on errors made. There was, however, a strong expression of feeling in the Seminar that there is no discontinuity between speech and writing. If this is so then it is no less 'natural' to read than to speak, and therefore what is required is for 'reading needs' to be discovered and stimulated.

Session 5 The particular points here related to the categories that had been set up to distinguish different kinds of children's writing. Are they theoretical categories or *ad hoc* ones? How do 'transactional' and 'expressive' differ, and what are their linguistic correlates? In any case are the categories the child's or the analyst's? Whatever the answer, the Seminar accepted that analysts should not be normative but should accept whatever writing children offer as good of its kind.

Session 6 In this summary session we were asked to re-formulate the problem. As the Chairman pointed out, the order of topics could have been reversed, with the more theoretical papers coming after the more practical ones, since the search for a necessary research application had indicated our lack of knowledge about linguistics in relation to language in use. The need for more work in this area was expressed by Bernstein in his notion of the Transmission–Acquisition Matrix. What he was in fact asking us to do was to accept that the separate disciplines had now stated their positions, and that we should look forward to a *joint* approach to language and learning in the 1974 Seminar.

It was inevitable in this summary session that we should come back to a number of earlier points. Among the more important ones were the two kinds of research advocated by Halliday, the straight linguistic type and the 'exploration' type. Such research might have something to say about the paucity of reading materials available to older children, paucity in the sense of a lack of variety. Why is it that in the secondary school there seems so little difference between the English of, say, History and Geography and even Chemistry?

And finally we were brought back to the central issue of this Seminar, the problem of inter-disciplinary communication, and the need for it. Our Chairman indicated the need to bring in the more sociological consideration of power and control which he felt were being ignored in a too narrowly psychological approach. And there the Seminar ended, having revealed the difficulty of inter-disciplinary communication and at the same time emphasised the value of attempting it.

I

Talking One's Way In

A Sociolinguistic Perspective on Language and Learning[1]

M. A. K. HALLIDAY

> If we ask of any form of communication the simple question what is being communicated, the answer is: information from the social system. The exchanges which are being communicated constitute the social system.
>
> MARY DOUGLAS[2]

The past fifteen years has witnessed an immense explosion in the work on language and learning, first from a psychological and more recently from a sociological standpoint. There has been a proliferation of studies of language acquisition and development; of language in the classroom; of speech varieties and their basis in the social structure; of attitudes to and prejudices against these varieties; of deficits and disadvantages and compensatory strategies of all kinds. Reading some of this material, one is left with an impression of vast confusion, a confusion that is as much moral as intellectual, in which little attempt is made to understand the other person's approach; one sums him up in a neat little epigram, calls him by a rude name, and leaves it at that. Anyone who hopes to contribute however modestly to the lessening of this confusion runs the risk of merely adding to it further. Yet one has to move forward; not merely because the work has been done, but because it embodies some extraordinarily penetrating insights, from which as they come together a coherent picture begins to emerge.

1. This paper is an attempt to contribute in a small way to the coming together. I shall try to trace one path through the maze, one that is perhaps less frequently trodden but which seems to pass through some of the major vantage points and in this way to link them one with another. I shall keep my eye fixed on one particular question, that of how language transmits culture. This

will serve as a linking theme for the attempt to bring into a theoretical relationship with one another a number of areas of rich resource that seem to have remained rather disconnected. How does a child learn, from the small change of everyday speech, the deeper patterns of the culture? How does the casual linguistic interaction of the home, the street and the neighbourhood initiate him into the mysteries of the social system—the social structure, systems of values, systems of knowledge and the like? Before he ever comes into school he has accumulated a great store of knowledge about all these things; not only without instruction, but without those from whom he has learnt it being aware that they know it themselves. And he has done nearly all of this through language.

Let me make it clear that I am not talking about how the child learns language, but about how he exploits language (in the course of learning it, to be sure) in the learning of other things—in the learning of the culture, in fact. We need to start perhaps from the notion of a social semiotic: of the culture as a semiotic system, or system of information—the latter term is perhaps more familiar, but I shall avoid it because it suggests a subjective or 'intra-organism' approach (the culture as 'what the member *knows*'), whereas I want to adopt an objective or 'inter-organism' approach, in terms of the meaning potential carried by the culture (and therefore what the member *can mean*, rather than what he knows). Somehow or other, but mainly through language, the child learns the meaning systems of the culture, he develops a social semiotic, and in the process becomes a member of the species 'social man'.

It is easy to cite linguistic instances showing this process at work. Here are a few, taken from my own 'sociolinguistic' study of language development; those taking part are Nigel, at age 2;11, his mother, his father, and an older child.

MOTHER (*having fetched Nigel home from school*): How on earth did you get all that sand in your hair? NIGEL: I was just standing up and I threw the sand to it [= 'at it'; referent unspecified] and it got in my hàir. MOTHER: And what did the teacher say? NIGEL: Nò . . . because it was time to go home and have your [= 'my'] pieces of meàt.

NIGEL (*to older child Nan who is playing with yoyo*): What's thàt? NAN: It's a yoyo. NIGEL: How does the string come ùp?

NAN: I don't know . . . you wind it down like that and it winds itself up again. (*Nigel is satisfied.*)

(*Nigel is watering the flowers, a great treat. He slaps some flowers with his hand.*) FATHER: I've told you three times not to slap the flowers, and if you do it again I'm going to turn the water off. NIGEL: But I don't wànt you to turn the wáter off so I'm nòt slapping the flówers any mòre. (*Father takes hose from him to direct it straight.*) NIGEL: (*protesting*): Nò! . . . I'm big enough to do it mysèlf!

NIGEL (*from playroom*): Mummy where are the ones with grèen in? MOTHER: The what? NIGEL: The àll green ones. MOTHER: But I don't know what it is you're talking about. NIGEL: The ones that I had in Nairòbi. (*Mother gives up.*)

NIGEL (*at teatime*): What day is it todày? MOTHER: It's Thursday. NIGEL: There's no schòol on Thursday. MOTHER: There is—you've already been to schòol. NIGEL: I mean . . . what comes after Thùrsday? MOTHER: Friday. There's school on Friday too. NIGEL: But you can't go to school on Friday yēt. MOTHER. No, it hasn't started being Friday yet.

Specimens such as these show very clearly how in the course of the most ordinary linguistic interaction the child is all the time learning the structure of the environment in which he is growing up, in all its aspects, material, logical, institutional and social. He is also at the same time developing his own unique personality, which is being formed at the intersection of a whole number of role relationships which are themselves likewise part of the semiotic structure of his universe. But it is one thing to recognise that all this is taking place, and that it is taking place through language; it is quite another thing to explain how language does it.

Let us use the word *text* to refer to any instance of language that is operational (as distinct from citational): everything that is said, or written, in some living context of use. Let us then conceive of text as choice. The text represents a selection within various sets of options; what is said presupposes a background of what might have been said but was not. In linguistic terms, it presupposes a paradigmatic environment: the choice of this implies the possibility of that and the other. These options are options in meaning; since our interest is in the meaning rather than in the wording, we can conceive of text not as 'what is said' but as 'what is meant', still in the environment of what might have been—'what might have been meant (but was not)'. A sociolinguistic description is a description of semantic options—an account of what can be meant, or in other words of a *meaning potential*. A text represents a pattern of selection within a meaning potential.

There are two ways of looking at the meaning potential. We may interpret it in the context of the situation, or we may interpret it in the context of the culture (to use Malinowski's all-important distinction). That is to say, we may think of the potential as being the whole semantic system of the language, or as being a specific sub-system (or set of sub-systems) that is associated with a particular class of situations, or contexts of use. The former is a fiction; we cannot describe the whole semantic system. The latter is also, of course, a fiction, but it is a more accessible one. We can represent the meaning potential in the form of sets of options that are specific to a given situation type.

In what follows we shall make use of the notion of text as semantic choice, and of meaning potential (the semantic systems within which the choice is made), in an attempt to throw a little more light on the question of how children learn about the culture through the language. Essentially they are learning one semiotic system through the medium of another one in which it is encoded. We shall try to identify the various components which make up the total picture of language as social interaction. Having considered each of the separate components in turn, we shall try to integrate them into a composite pattern.

2. First of all there is the *text*, the actual instances of linguistic interaction in which the child is in one way or another involved. It should not be forgotten that he listens to a vast quantity of text in the form of dialogue in which he is not himself a participant. (It was at 3;1 that Nigel began formulating the distinction between participant and onlooker, asking frequently *Were you saying that to me?*) Where he is a participant he is, of course, co-author of the text.

Secondly, there is the *situation*, the medium within which the text lives and breathes. This is exactly the Malinowskian concept of 'context of situation', as made explicit and modified by Firth, who pointed out that it had to be seen not as an aggregate of concrete spatiotemporal goings-on, a sort of backdrop of sights and sounds, but as an abstract representation of the relevant environment. In modern jargon, it is the ecology of the text. It is a characteristic of the adult language system that the text it engenders is not tied to the immediate scenario as its environment. The context of situation may be entirely remote from what is happening around the act of speaking or writing.

Thirdly there is the semantic variety, or *register*, of which the text may be regarded as an instance. This is a configuration of meanings that is typically associated with a particular class of situations; the semantic resources that are characteristically deployed in social contexts of the given type. Essentially it is a range of meaning potential—of sets of options that are 'at risk' under the given situational conditions.

Fourthly, there is the *linguistic system* itself. In the present context what concerns us most is the semantic system, but the semantic system considered not from a conceptual but from a functional point of view, and in particular its organisation into basic components of a functional kind. We shall recognise three such components: ideational, interpersonal, and textual. The first is the speaker's meaning potential as an observer; it is the content function of language, language as about something. The second is his meaning potential as an intruder: it is the participatory function of language, language as doing something. The third is the text-forming potential, that which makes language relevant. In fact these are formal as well as functional components, because they constitute the basic organising principle of the lexicogrammatical system; this is what enables—and disposes—the child to learn the lexicogrammar: since the system is organised along functional lines, it relates clearly to what the child can see language doing as he observes it going on around him.[3]

Finally there is the *social structure*. (We use the term 'social system' in a wider sense, in which it encompasses all the elements that we are talking about.) This enters the picture in two ways. It is a part of the environment, and hence a part of what is being transmitted to the child through language. It is also a determinant of the transmission process, since it determines the rôle relationship in the family and other socialising agencies, and so creates the conditions of the child's learning. Our understanding of how this happens is due to Bernstein, who has demonstrated that the social structure is not merely an ornamental backdrop to linguistic interaction, as linguists have tended to think of it, but an essential element in the deeper processes that are involved.[4]

If a child learns the culture from ordinary everyday linguistic interaction, as he certainly does, we must suppose not only that he decodes correctly in a way that is specifically relevant to the context of situation but also that he interprets correctly in a way that is generally relevant to the context of culture. In other words, if his mother tells him off he not only knows that he is being told off but also learns something about the value systems of the culture he is participating in. This presupposes that the linguistic system must be coherent not only within itself but also with the culture; not only are the semantic options which make up the meaning potential *realised* explicitly in the lexicogrammar—they are also themselves *realising* the higher-order meanings of the social semiotic. All the elements mentioned above play some part in the total picture.

3. From a sociological point of view a text is meaningful not so much because we do not know what the speaker is going to say, as in a mathematical model of communication, as because we do know. Given certain facts we can predict a great deal of what he is going to say with a significantly high probability of being right. (Those who place a high value on the creativity of language may be reassured that his behaviour is none the less creative even if our predictions are fulfilled to the letter.) The 'certain facts' are the general properties of the situation, in the abstract sense in which the term is being used here. There are many ways of representing these; one of the best known is Hymes' list of categories which we may summarise as form and content, setting, participants, ends (intent and effect), key, medium, genre, and interactional norms.[5] The problem has always been to know what kind of theoretical validity to accord to categories of this kind. We have to think in terms not of 'a situation', but of a general social context, or situation type. The situational factors are constitutive of the text. They specify the register, the semantic configurations which characterise text in that type of situation—the meanings the speaker will typically draw on.

As always, such categories are two-faced. If we set up a conceptual framework for the representation of situation types, it is not enough that the categories used serve to predict features of the text. They also relate 'upwards' to a higher order of abstraction: in this case, two such higher orders, the social and the linguistic. They must be interpretable not only in terms of the culture but also in terms of the linguistic system. It is the latter requirement in particular that may lead us to select from among the many existing and possible schemes; and we shall return to one proposed some years ago by Halliday, McIntosh and Strevens, a threefold analysis in terms of the concepts of *field*, *mode* and *tenor*.[6] It was

not entirely clear at the time why such a scheme should be pre-
ferred, except that intuitively it seemed simpler than most others.
But we can now see that it provides an essential link between the
linguistic system and the text.

There have been a number of more recent discussions of the
concepts of field, mode and tenor.[7] A situation type, or social
context, as understood here, is characterised by a semiotic structure,
a complex of features which sets it apart from other situation
types. This structure is interpreted on three dimensions: in terms
of the ongoing activity, the role relationships involved, and the
rhetorical channel. The first of these, the field, corresponds
roughly to Hymes' 'setting' and 'ends'; it is the field of action of
the participants in which the text is functioning, including the
'subject-matter' as a special case. The second, the tenor, which
corresponds in general terms to Hymes' 'participants' and 'key',
refers to the role relationships among the participants in the situation, including speech styles or levels of formality but also much
else besides. The mode, roughly Hymes' 'instrumentalities' and
'genre', is the channel or wave-length selected, which itself is a
matter of the part that is assigned to language in the situation;
it includes the distinction between speech and writing, which is
interpreted as a function of the rhetorical mode. These are not
kinds of language use, nor are they simply generalised components
of the speech situation. They are the environmental determinants
of text. Given an adequate specification of field, tenor and mode,
we can make certain predictions about the linguistic properties
of the text associated with that situation type: that is, about the
register, the configurations of semantic options that typically
feature in this environment, and hence about the grammar and
vocabulary, which are the realisations of the semantic options.

The possibility of making such predictions arises because the
categories of field, tenor and mode, which we use to characterise
the semiotic structure of the situation, are in their turn associated
with the functional components of the semantic system. This is not,
of course, a coincidence; the semantic system evolved, we may
assume, operationally, as a form of symbolic interaction in social
contexts, so it is not unexpected that it should reflect the structure
of such contexts in its own internal organisation. We referred
above to the tripartite functional composition of the semantic
system, with its components of ideational, interpersonal, and
textual. (It should be mentioned, perhaps, that this scheme is
not something that is arrived at from the outside. The tripartite

organisation is very clearly present in the lexicogrammatical system of natural languages—for example, the threefold structuring of the clause in terms of transitivity, mood and theme.) It appears that each of the different components of meaning is typically activated by the corresponding feature of the situation. Thus, the *field* is associated with the *ideational* component, the *tenor* with the *interpersonal* component, and the *mode* with the *textual* component.

Let us take another textual example, this time from Nigel at age 1;11.

MOTHER (*in bathroom, Nigel sitting on chair*): Now you wait there till I get your face-cloth. Keep sitting there. (*But Nigel is already standing up on the chair.*) NIGEL (*in exact imitation of mother's intonation pattern, not in a correcting intonation*): Keep standing thére. Put the mug on the flóor. MOTHER: Put the mug on the floor? What do you want? NIGEL: Daddy tòothbrush. MOTHER: Oh you want Daddy's toothbrush do you? NIGEL: Yés . . . you [= I] want to put the fròg in the múg. MOTHER: I think the frog is too big for the mug. NIGEL: Yes you can put the dùck in the múg . . . make bùbble . . . make bùbble. MOTHER: To-morrow. Nearly all the water's run out. NIGEL: You want Mummy red tóothbrush . . . yes you can have Mummy old red tóothbrush.

We might identify the situational features in some such terms as the following:

Field: Personal toilet, assisted [mother washing child]; concurrently [child] exploring (i) container principle (i.e. putting things in things) and (ii) ownership and acquisition of property (i.e. getting things that belong to other people)
Tenor: Mother and small child interaction; mother determining course of action; child pursuing own interests, seeking permission; mother granting permission and sharing the child's interests, but keeping her own course in view
Mode: Spoken dialogue; pragmatic speech ('language-in-action'), the mother's guiding, the child's furthering (accompanying or immediately preceding) the actions to which it is appropriate; cooperative, without conflict of goals

Looking at the text, we find that the field tends to determine the transitivity patterns—the types of process, e.g. relational clauses, possessive (*get, have*) and circumstantial: locative (*put*), material process clauses, spatial: posture (*sit, stand*); also the minor processes, e.g. circumstantial: locative (*in*); perhaps the tenses (simple present); and the *content* aspect of the vocabulary, e.g. naming of objects. All these belong to the ideational component of the semantic system.

The tenor tends to determine the patterns of mood, e.g. [mother] imperative (*you wait, keep sitting*) and of modality, e.g. [child] permission (*want to, can,* and non-finite forms such as *make bubble* meaning 'I want to be allowed to . . .'); also of person, e.g. [mother] 'second person' (*you*), [child] 'first person' (you [= I]), and of key, represented by the system of intonation (pitch contour, e.g. child's systematic opposition of rising, demanding a response, versus falling, not demanding a response). These are all part of the interpersonal component.

The mode tends to determine the forms of cohesion, e.g. question-and-answer with the associated type of ellipsis (*What do you want?—Daddy toothbrush*); the patterns of voice and theme, e.g. active voice with child as subject/theme; the forms of deixis, e.g. exophoric [situation-referring] *the*; and the lexical continuity, e.g. repetition of *mug, toothbrush, put in.* All these fall within the textual component of the semantics.

Thus there is a general tendency for the different elements in the context of situation to call on different areas in the meaning potential, and hence in turn on the different parts of the lexico-grammatical system through which the meanings are realised.

4. Bernstein's work has demonstrated that the semantic configurations which are typically associated with a given situation type in a given culture may vary in a way that is not random but is related to the social structure. In certain 'key' contexts, situation types that are critical for social learning, different people have different habits of meaning. These are not just matters of individual psychology; they are related to social factors, and particularly, it appears, to the type of family role structure. Since the type of family structure is to a certain extent a function of social class, the variation in semiotic style is also, to a certain extent, a function of social class. This is not really surprising, once we are prepared to recognise that in pluralistic societies there may be differences of class ideology; this itself is sub-cultural variation of a semiotic kind, and there is no reason to reject the possibility that this might be reflected in certain different ways of meaning, or semantic styles.

There is no need to assume here that different sub-cultures have different semantic systems. It is conceivable that they might; regional dialects often do differ at certain points in their semantic systems, usually in relatively minor ways, and it is not to be ruled out *a priori* that there might be minor differences also between sub-cultural dialects. But this is not what we are talking about. We are not considering an idealised semantic system in isolation from social contexts, but rather networks of semantic options that are specific to the situation type. There is variety among speakers in the range of meanings they typically deploy in particular situation types; and this variety is a function of the social structure.

Bernstein has given a name to the principle which regulates this variety; he calls it the *code*. Essentially the code is the controlling principle of semiotic organisation. Bernstein finds a small number of very general variables lying behind the diversity of meaning habits: the two which have figured most prominently in his work are those of elaboration and orientation. Each one of these is itself a complex of variables, among which there is a tendency to co-vary. An elaborated variant is one in which the meanings tend towards a more universalistic 'mode' (less ambiguity in the situational reference) and a more discretionary 'tenor' (more ambiguity in the role relationships). The first of these is likely to be reflected in the textual component, the second in the inter-personal component. Orientation may be towards persons or towards objects; it is likely to be reflected in the ideational component, and perhaps also in the interpersonal, since a person type of orientation may reveal itself in the speaker's own com-municative role patterns.

Empirical studies have shown these differential semantic tendencies at work in various instances of critical contexts, for example the mother's regulation of the behaviour of her child. The differences show a correlation with social class. (We have pointed out above that the link with social class is an indirect one, via the family role system; but social class can be objectively controlled, for purposes of investigation, whereas family type cannot.) Let us give a brief illustration of this. Ruqaiya Hasan, in her analysis of stories told by young children, has found differences correlating significantly with sex, with social class, and with both taken together. For example, as regards the internal cohesion of the text, which forms part of the textual component in the seman-tic system, the middle-class children show a greater use of anaphoric ties (references to the text) and a lesser use of exophoric ties (references to the situation); they also show a lesser tendency towards the use of cohesive chains which are non-continuous (in which the cohesive tie shifts from one referent to another, as opposed to continuing with the same referent). Girls tend to make longer cohesive chains than boys do, and to make less use of simple successive relations (the temporal sequence of events) in the narrative. It is worth noting, incidentally, that Ruqaiya Hasan's findings bear out Bernstein's repeated assertion that the difference of code elaboration has nothing to do with poverty or richness of linguistic resources. Neither class, and neither sex, is linguistically deprived.[9]

As an example of the range of meaning potential that is associated with a specific social context, and of how it may be represented as a network of options, Figure 1 (p. 22) gives a summary of an analysis by Geoffrey Turner of the results of an investigation of the meaning patterns displayed by mothers of young children in a regulative situation. Jenny Cook-Gumperz assembled a large quantity of material and analysed and interpreted it from a sociological point of view, with important results for the understanding of patterns of social control.[10] Turner took a part of the same material and worked on it using linguistic methods, corroborating Jenny Cook-Gumperz' results and also adding to them, since he was able to organise some of the material in semantic networks and subject it to a more delicate analysis. Figure 1 is based on one of Turner's studies.[11] I have modified it to give a more systematic presentation in a short space, and made minor changes in interpretation. It shows the meaning potential that is embodied in the mothers' responses to questions about how they would deal with certain specific situations that might arise requiring some attention to the child's behaviour.

A network of this kind has two important properties: it is two-faced, and it is open-ended. It is open-ended in the sense that each of the terminal options in the network is a potential point of entry into a further, more delicate choice; there is no limit to the differentiation in meaning that may be recognised. It is two-faced in that a semantic system is an interface between language and the non-linguistic universe; it is the encoding, or realisation, of a fragment of the social semiotic into a system of meanings that is then recoded, or realised in turn, at the heart of the linguistic system, in patterns of grammar and vocabulary. The second point needs expanding briefly.

The network is an abstract representation of the range of possible meanings. What the child actually hears from the mother are sentences like *I'm not going to buy you anything, that was very naughty of you* or *you mustn't do that, it's stealing*. Such sentences contain within themselves the lexicogrammatical realisation of the categories of the network; and it is a principle of systemic theory that each option makes some contribution to the lexicogrammatical shape (which may be a 'null' contribution where this is in contrast to something else). Hence it is not unreasonable to assert that the utterance is decoded into something like these meanings—note that the claim that the child decodes successfully is implicit in any theory of social learning. What we are trying to do here is to make this claim explicit. Something of how this works can be seen from Figure 2 (p. 23), which gives the realisations of the options of part of the network in Figure 1; Figure 2 is again based on Turner but modified a little for the present purpose.

At the same time the network faces 'upwards'. When the child hears his mother say *you mustn't do that, it's stealing* he not only decodes it as a form of control on his behaviour but also learns from it about the value systems of the culture. The semantic options, while themselves realised through selections in the lexicogrammatical system, or 'words-in-structures', are at the same time the realisation of a higher-level semiotic; and this includes not only the semiotic structure of the particular situation type (the context of situation, in its organisation as field, tenor and mode) but also the total set of possible situation types, or social contexts, that constitutes the culture—the social semiotic, as we referred to it above. Linguistically, as we saw, this is made possible by the functional organisation of the semantic system of natural languages, whereby the specific categories of the context of situation activate corresponding but at the same time highly generalised choices in meaning. So the child learns to move easily between the context of situation and the context of culture (and his *language* learning can in fact be looked at in this light).

In the process, the child takes over the *codes*. The social semiotic is transmitted to him through the filtering effect of organising principles that define the sub-culture of which he is himself a part. As he learns the culture, he also learns the code—the grid, or particular sub-cultural angle on the social system. The child's linguistic experience reveals the culture to him through the code, and so transmits the code as part of the culture.

5. Figure 3 (p. 24) suggests in a diagrammatic form how the components of the puzzle may be fitted together. The orderly arrangement of words-in-structures that makes up everyday

linguistic interaction, which we are calling the *text*, is the product (and realisation) of a large number of more or less simultaneous choices in meaning. It is embedded in a context of situation, which is an instance of a *situation type*, or social context. The situation type has a systematic structure in terms of the general categories of *field, tenor* and *mode*—the type of activity, the rôle relationships, and the rhetorical functions assigned to language within it. These categories are related to the functional components of the adult *semantic system, ideational, interpersonal* and *textual*—meaning as content (the observer function), as participation (the intruder function) and as texture (the relevance function, without which the other two are sterile). The semiotic structure of the particular situation type, its specific pattern of field, tenor and mode, resonates, as it were, in the semantic system, activating small networks of semantic options to create a meaning potential that is specific to that situation type; this produces a particular semantic configuration, or register, which we recognise as the speech variant typically associated with the situation type in question. This process is in turn controlled by the *code*, the mode of semiotic organisation, or meaning style, that represents the particular sub-cultural angle on the social system. This angle of vision is itself a function of the social structure, reflecting among other things the pattern of social hierarchy, for example (perhaps typically) through family types and family rôle systems.

A sociolinguistic approach to language and learning seeks to bring together the various components of the process whereby a child learns through language in social contexts. Just as, following Mary Douglas, in any communication process what is being communicated is information from the social system, so in any learning process what is being learnt is information from the social system. As we put it earlier, the child is learning the social semiotic. The meaning potential that he is building up *is* the culture; hence it is sensitive to, and so interpretable in, the contexts of the culture.

We should not be too surprised, as some linguists seem to have been, that a child can learn his language. The linguistic interaction with which he is surrounded is rich and highly structured; what is more, it is contextualised—it is text-in-situation. We must not forget that the child himself is in the middle of the diagram. He has abundant evidence not only for learning the linguistic system but also for learning to free language from the constraints of the immediate situation. His language learning consists in building up the context of culture, the social semiotic, from countless particular contexts of situation, or semiotic events.

His goal is often defined in sociolinguistics as a form of competence: a communicative competence, an ability to produce sentences that are situationally appropriate. But, quite apart from the restrictive nature of this definition, the concept of competence, with its idealised speaker–hearer, is very unhelpful in a sociolinguistic perspective (even if we replace him by an idealised meaner). Hymes has done a great deal to disentangle the confusion into which that concept has led us, especially with his distinction of what is formally possible, what is ('psycholinguistically') feasible, what is ('sociolinguistically') appropriate, and what is actually done.[12] But essentially the competence approach imposes an 'intra-organism' perspective; it treats the individual as an assemblage of parts, and interprets linguistic interaction in terms of what goes on inside his head. This is merely adding an unnecessary unknown; why not keep to the 'inter-organism' standpoint, treating the individual as a whole in interaction with other individuals, and go straight on to consider his potential for meaning, which is the potential he derives from the social system? We then have a view of sociolinguistic variation in which it has nothing to do with native wit (and therefore questions of genetic differences between groups do not even arise—there is no place for them in linguistics) but is a function of variation in the social structure. All human beings are endowed with the ability to learn the social semiotic; but semiotic systems differ, and sometimes they clash, which is when the child finds himself in difficulties—his own semiotic is at variance with the received semiotic of the culture.

The essential feature of a theoretical approach to questions of language and learning is that it is based on some interpretation of meaning in language. As Hymes says, 'A theory of the sort needed here starts with social life and looks in at language; thus functions guide, structures follow'—we might add 'social life *and the social structure*'. Linguistic structure, the internal workings of the language system, will appear as derived, as the form of realisation of linguistic meanings; and linguistic meanings are themselves the realisation of social meanings. Meaning is a specifically human activity, and we are doing it most of the time. What makes it possible for a child to learn through language is essentially the fact that language enables him to mean.

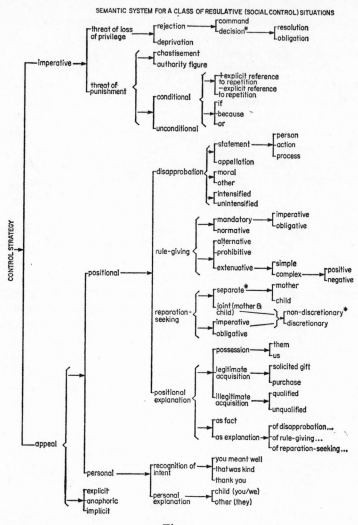

SEMANTIC SYSTEM FOR A CLASS OF REGULATIVE (SOCIAL CONTROL) SITUATIONS

Figure 1

Test Situations

What would you do if —— brought you a bunch of flowers and you
found out that he/she had got them from a neighbour's garden?
Imagine —— had been out shopping with you and when you came
home you found he/she'd picked up some little thing from one of
the counters without your noticing. What would you say or do?

Based on Geoffrey J. Turner, 'Social class differences in the behaviour
of mothers in regulative (social control) situations', University of London Institute of Education, Sociological Research Unit (forthcoming).

Figure 2

LEXICOGRAMMATICAL REALISATIONS OF SOME CATEGORIES
OF 'CONTROL STRATEGY' (see Figure 1, 'imperative')
Numbers following R refer to numbered paragraphs in *Roget's Thesaurus*.
Abridged Edition 1953. * = typical form

Threat of Loss of Privilege

Rejection: material process ('Departure', R 293; 'Recession', R 287); Hearer *you* = Medium: positive

Deprivation: material process: benefactive ('Giving', R 784); Hearer *you* = Beneficiary (Recipient/Client); negative

Command: middle; imperative: jussive: exclusive
Ex.: you go on upstairs; go up to bed now

Decision: indicative: declarative [*either* middle *or* non-middle: active/passive, Speaker *I* = Agent (optional in passive); middle* if rejective, non-middle* if deprivation]

Resolution: future/: in present/present in present
Ex.: you're going upstairs; I'll take/I'm taking you upstairs [rejection]; I'm not going to buy you anything; you're not going to be given a sweet [deprivation]

Obligation: modulation: passive: necessity
Ex.: I'll have to take you upstairs; you'll have to go upstairs [rejection]; you won't have to have a sweet; I shan't be able to give you a sweet; next time you won't be able to go shopping with me [deprivation]

Threat of Punishment

Chastisement: material process ('Punishment', R 972); Hearer *you* = Medium; non-middle: active*, Speaker *I* = Agent; indicative: declarative; future/: in present; positive
Ex.: I'll smack you; you'll get smacked

Authority figure: material process ('Punishment', R 972; 'Disapprobation', R 932 [paras. beginning *reprehend* . . . sense of 'verbal punishment']; Hearer *you* = Medium; non-middle; 3rd person (father*, policeman*) = Agent; indicative: declarative; future/: in present; positive
Ex.: the policeman will tell you off; Daddy'll smack you

Conditional: 'you do that'
'if':   hypotactic; condition in dependent clause, threat in main clause
Ex.: if you do that, . . .

'because':   hypotactic; condition in main clause, threat in dependent clause
Ex.: don't/you mustn't do that because . . .

'or':   paratactic; condition in clause 1, threat in clause 2
                         Ex.: don't/you mustn't do that or . . .
explicit   *again* in condition [/*next time* = *if* . . . *again*]
reference to   *Ex.:* if you do that again, . . .; next time you do that . . .;
repetition: don't do that again because/or . . .

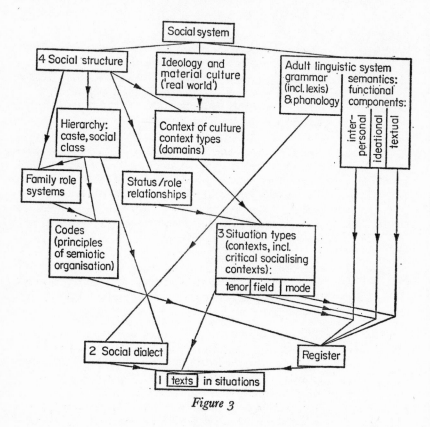

Figure 3

NOTES

1. This paper was prepared during my tenure of a fellowship at the Center for Advanced Study in the Behavioral Sciences, Stanford, California. I should like to express my thanks to the Center for the opportunities this has afforded.

2. Douglas, Mary, 'Do dogs laugh? a cross-cultural approach to body symbolism', *Journal of Psychosomatic Research,* **15,** p. 389.

3. Cf. Halliday, M. A. K., 'Learning how to mean', in Eric and Elizabeth Lenneberg (eds.), *Foundations of Language Development: a*

multidisciplinary approach, UNESCO & IBRO (International Brain Research Organization), in press; also Halliday, M. A. K., *Explorations in the Functions of Language*, Edward Arnold (Explorations in Language Study), London 1973, passim. The first component corresponds in general to what Hymes calls 'referential', the second to his 'social', 'stylistic' or 'socio-expressive'; see Hymes, Dell H., 'Linguistic theory and the functions of speech', *International Days of Sociolinguistics*, Rome 1969. The third corresponds to, or rather includes, the 'functional sentence perspective' of the Prague School linguistic theory.

4. Cf. Bernstein, Basil, *Class, Codes and Control. Vol. I: Theoretical studies towards a sociology of language*, Routledge & Kegan Paul (Primary Socialisation, Language & Education), London 1971, p. 123: 'The thesis to be developed here places the emphasis on changes in the social structure as major factors in shaping or changing a given culture through their effect on the consequences of fashions of speaking'.

5. See Hymes, Dell H., 'Models of interaction of language and social setting', *Journal of Social Issues*, **23**, 1967.

6. Halliday, M. A. K., McIntosh, Angus, and Strevens, Peter, *The Linguistic Sciences and Language Teaching*, Longman (Longman's Linguistics Library), London 1964; Indiana University Press, Bloomington, Ind., Chapter 4.

7. See for example Doughty, Peter, Pearce, John, and Thornton, Geoffrey, *Exploring Language*, Edward Arnold, London 1972, esp. Chapter 11; Halliday, M. A. K., *Language and Social Man*, Longman (Papers of the Programme in Linguistics and English Teaching, Second Series), London, in press. Cf. also Ure, Jean, and Ellis, Jeffrey, 'Register in descriptive linguistics and linguistic sociology', in Oscar Uribe Villegas (ed.), *Las concepciones y problemas actuales de la sociolingüística*, University of Mexico Press, Mexico City 1972.

8. For the child's linguistic system at this stage see 'Learning how to mean'; for the relation of different lexicogrammatical systems to the functional components of the semantics see *Explorations in the Functions of Language*, Chapter 5, Table 1 (both references as in n. 3 above).

9. See Hasan, Ruqaiya, *Language in the Imaginative Context: a sociolinguistic study of stories told by children*, Routledge & Kegan Paul (Primary Socialisation, Language & Education), London, forthcoming.

10. Cook-Gumperz, Jenny, *Socialisation and Social Control: a study of social class differences in the language of maternal control*, Routledge & Kegan Paul (Primary Socialisation, Language & Education), London 1973.

11. Turner, Geoffrey J., 'Social class differences in the behaviour of mothers in regulative (social control) situations', University of

London Institute of Education, Sociological Research Unit, forthcoming.

12. Hymes, Dell H., 'Competence and performance in linguistic theory', in Renira Huxley and Elisabeth Ingram (eds.), *Language Acquisition: Models and Methods*, Academic Press, London and New York 1971, p. 23.

SPEAKER'S INTRODUCTION

The invitation to take part in this seminar posed a problem because I had just finished writing for a different occasion the paper which could have been very suitable for this seminar—except that it turned out to be about a hundred pages long. This was a paper which I had put into a series associated with the work that I was doing for a number of years in London in the Programme in Linguistics and English Teaching, work which led to the production of materials for primary and secondary level work on language in schools. The 100-page-long paper is called 'Language and Social Man' and is an attempt at what would be called nowadays in current jargon *ecology of language*. It is a kind of social ecology of language and what the teacher can do about it.[1]

What I was trying to do in that paper was to look at the functions of language for the child, against a general perspective on language and learning interpreted particularly in the sense of how the child is socialised through language. Then I tried to suggest a number of areas of exploration which the teacher, together with his students (of whatever age), could investigate in the classroom.

In thinking about this seminar it seemed to me that some kind of a theoretical sociolinguistic background was needed. (I myself am not sure what sociolinguistic means any more; I suppose I have really been doing sociolinguistics all my life, except that I have always called it linguistics.) A mass of important work has been done in the sociolinguistic field during the last decade. There must be ten or twelve different areas but no general theory of the social conditions of language use, as Dell Hymes said at a previous Edinburgh conference[2]. What I have tried to do, therefore, in this short paper is to sketch some kind of sociolinguistic model of learning through language, trying to link those areas together. [*Halliday then referred to Figure 3, page 24, in his paper.*] Let me try to provide a guide through a part of this diagram. The main linking box is the one at the foot of the page; it is—

1. *Text* that brings everything together. It is true that a great deal of work has been going on recently in text studies, but in none of it are we given any clear indication how our relations of actual linguistic interaction can be seen to be the expression of the underlying actions that we claim are going on at the time. A good example is the work of

Sachs and Schegloff, influenced by symbolic interaction coming from Goffman through ethnomethodology. This is very good but it studies minutiae of social interaction with no reference to linguistic theory.

2. *Social dialect studies*, e.g. Labov. We are given insights into social and urban dialects but Labov stops short at the semantic system. Of course there is no semantics in what he does since he generally works with a two-level model of language—phonology and morphology. Until we face up to the question: 'Are there or can there be differences between social dialects at the semantic level?' (which Labov does *not* ask), we cannot embed the work on social dialect into a wider perspective of language and learning.

3. *Situation type studies*, e.g. Hymes on the ethnography of speaking. These are valuable but we could all write down such lists out of our heads and we have no way of preferring one to another.

4. At the top of the diagram on the left we have *social structure* and the derived variables. Here we have the work of Basil Bernstein who is the only social theorist who has insisted on language as an essential component in the picture that he is building up. The problem was to relate his work to the linguistic system as a whole and, at the same time, to the text. His own colleagues in the sociological research unit have now been showing over the past year how his own theories are made explicit and are realised through the text. They have been doing so through the methods of lexicogrammatical and semantic analysis. What is needed now is the relation of this to the linguistic system as a whole.

In my paper I have tried to put these components together and to suggest that there are certain points of contact which do, at least tentatively, suggest some kind of model. The *social dialect*, the *code* (in Bernstein's sense), *variety* (in terms of register), the *individual*, the *speech event*, the *semantic system*, and the *social system* can all then be discussed under the same heading. I have provided illustrations of this linking model by drawing on the work of Geoffrey Turner and of my wife, Ruqaiya Hasan, and her current work on language in the imaginative context, a study of stories told by children.

[*Halliday then referred to John Reagan's letter which had just arrived with comments on his paper. John Reagan had been invited to attend the Seminar but had been prevented. The relevant part of his letter follows.*]

1. Using Halliday's model regarding the environmental determinants of text, how would a variation in the specification of field, tenor and mode within the classroom correlate with the linguistic properties associated with the respective situational types? More specifically, assuming that some aspects of field, mode and tenor will remain constant in most classroom situations, which aspects of these three criteria will bear most significantly on a variation in the text?

2(*a*). Allowing that educational and classroom structure is in some measure a sub-component of a larger cultural system, how might we begin to describe systematically the unique features of the semantic configurational sub-system within the context of the larger cultural system? Can we distinguish the semantic configurations inherent in the classroom from those which are a function of education in the transmission of culture?

(*b*) Does classroom discourse have any special variation as compared to discourse-at-large? Is this simply a matter of exactness of analysis? Is there a special classroom, perhaps class-by-class, semiotic similar in position to classroom discourse as the cultural semiotic is to speech in general?

3. The opportunity should not be overlooked to increase the teacher's awareness of the variety of language functions and message types used by adults to inform and control children which appears to be an important practical consequence of Bernstein's remarks on language use, social class, and cultural transmission.

Notes

1. Halliday, M. A. K., *Language and Social Man*, Longman (Papers of the Programme in Linguistics and English Teaching, Second Series), London, in press.
2. Hymes, Dell H., 'Competence and performance in linguistic theory', in Renira Huxley and Elisabeth Ingram (eds.), *Language Acquisition: Models and Methods*, Academic Press, London and New York 1971.

Discussant: *Clive Criper*

I shall start by trying to restate what I take to be the underlying argument of this paper, first looking at it theoretically and then moving on to the practical implications for language teaching and learning and actual behaviour in the classroom.

The crucial underlying theme of the paper is, I suggest, the process by which language transmits culture. As Halliday asks: 'How does the child learn the patterns of his culture from the small change of everyday speech?' Primacy, then, is given to language here. Culture is defined in terms of a common meaning system so that as observers we are looking in at a society and seeing what range of meanings are available to people in that society. 'What semantic options are open?' as he puts it. This represents a paradigmatic kind of approach, viz. what range of alternatives are there in society, and these alternatives are, I want to stress, alternatives within the *whole* society; they are not necessarily all available to every individual.

Now in the process of learning, so the paper argues, the social structure of society determines in some way the rôle relationships that, for example, are in the family system. These in turn, one can say, determine the semantic variety of the language that the child will acquire. The structure of this variety of language, or register, which is what the child acquires, directly reflects the functions that the language actually fulfils in communication, in the set of situations in which it occurs. In other words, language operates functionally in a social sense, and this is directly reflected within the actual linguistic structure of the variety concerned. Hence, in the diagram, these direct equations between terms like field, tenor and mode on the one hand, and certain characteristics of the code on the other, e.g. mood, theme, notions of this kind.

This paper, then, represents a rare attempt to fit together almost as reflections of each other, notions of social structure and its connections to the family system, to social class, to register, etc. Again speech functions from a sociological point of view are related to functions of the code (and I am using code here in the sense of *grammatical* code, not in the Bernstein sense).

I hope the Seminar will not get bogged down in terminologies and the difficulties of reconciling one set of terminologies to another. What I want to do is to make two main points and then some minor ones.

First, while it is understandable that all of us here wish to emphasise the importance of language, I think there is an overemphasis on language in this paper—and perhaps in some of the others too—in the way in which it states that language use is almost the only way of socialising a child, in particular within the home. I suggest that we should not claim that all socialisation comes through language and language alone; that there are, in fact, other actions, other behaviours that have equal validity in the process of socialising. Let us look at language from a social point of view but don't let's pretend it is the only factor which is likely to affect education and educational chances.

Second, the theoretical ground underlying the argument running through the paper is one of functionalism—in a fairly extreme form. Such a view may well be—or it certainly has been in anthropology and sociology—an extremely useful heuristic device for forcing field workers and students to look at the interconnections between what is going on. But the dangers are that it leads to a somewhat static kind of model. This is precisely my fear in connection with Halliday's paper. The functionalist approach prevents him, I suggest, from bringing into focus the crucial things that I suppose we should be concerned with, and these things are social change and conflict.

For example, when we talk about separate registers (assuming for the moment registers are separate entities) and idealise the data in such a way that we assume some sort of uniformity within these registers, we are forcing ourselves to take up a static position. But it is precisely conflict of one kind or another that we should be actually interested in, even within, for example, the work of Basil Bernstein that Halliday quotes, where one looks at the evidence of socialisation within the family and the importance of the family system in determining children's outlook, their semantic system. While the mother has a crucial importance within the family, we need to consider the possibility of conflict of use and of values within the family, of differences between mother, father, other siblings, etc. Similarly in the school, we may find conflicting interests between, say, peer group in school and peer group in the street, and again in the formal classroom situation. As I see it then, one task of this Seminar is to see where the misfits are, rather than where there are perfect correlations and goodness of fit.

Third, there is another area we might consider. Is it useful to attempt to establish language varieties or registers as such as separate entities rather than attempt to look at register differences? In other words, to follow the Labov-type work of attempting to investigate within the local situation what are the crucially differentiating variables of a sociolinguistic nature, within Scotland, Edinburgh, Glasgow, wherever.

Fourth, the notion of function. Two kinds of speech function have been mentioned; the sociologist's speech functions, in the sense of how does language actually operate in an interaction; and the linguist's speech functions, those found within the linguistic code. I would like to pose the question—should we really expect to find a close connection between these two kinds of function? Should we not, perhaps, pay more attention to what we might call pragmatics, where there is no direct one-to-one connection between the grammatical form and what is actually meant by the individual in the particular social stituation; for example, the old saw of how many ways there are of giving an order. How does one look at the connections between linguistic form and function in the broad sense?

Fifth, I think we need to come down from the area of semantics to the lower levels of language in order to interpret what is happening. It seems to me that in linguistics itself semantics is a very confused and confusing area in which it is extremely difficult to talk systematically and meaningfully. And I believe the same is true in sociology. When people start talking about meaning (in ethnomethodology, for example) they become immersed in generalities. Can we, in fact, cope with such large questions as linguistic deprivation; does it imply some kind of semiotic deprivation? What would that mean and how could we translate it into some kind of operational research? Semantics and the semiotic, these are useful theoretical devices for bringing together a whole number of areas but I suspect we shall want to come down to a more specific area.

GENERAL DISCUSSION

Margaret Donaldson I think that questions concerning what semantic options are open or how language operates in an interaction are extremely important. But I do not know how one begins to answer them

when they are in so general a form. At the same time I feel very strongly
that what we need at the moment is a study of semantics. I would feel
uneasy about any suggestion that we evade problems of meaning
because they are too difficult, but I would like to see the problems
sharpened and made much more precise. We cannot all at one go answer
questions such as what semantic options are open. But in narrow and
more limited areas we can work at questions of how children come to
comprehend meaning in language.

Joan Tough I cannot find in Halliday's paper anything that comes
close to what I see as the relationship which is set up in an interaction—
which I take to be the source of meaning. Nor can I agree with Criper
about different ways of giving an order. Different message forms convey
quite different meanings, and it is the relationship which is in the mind
of the sender which determines the particular variety he selects.

Halliday I agree with Clive Criper that I have overemphasised
language; that was deliberate. The main problem we are concerned
with is, I think, how to relate the semantic system (outside language)
to some high-level semiotic. This is where the linguists have lagged
behind. We have not done our jobs. We have not given a central role to
the interpretation of semantics. I agree with Margaret Donaldson's
perspective here. Now a point about register. I think I am responsible
for confusion here. Let me try to put this straight: I do not regard
registers as entities in themselves at all. My own early register model,
like my thinking altogether at that stage, was much too much embedded
in the lexicogrammatical system. I *did* think of a register as a set of
lexicogrammatical features. I think now this was *wrong*. It should be
seen rather as a semantic configuration. Now I do not think that the
child is socialised into certain registers as entities. What I *do* think is
that we need an intermediate level between the linguistic system on the
one hand and Bernstein's codes (which I interpret as the principles of
semiotic organisation deriving from the social structure) on the other.
It is this intermediate level that I call a register. As to Criper's point
about looking at points of conflict, I am a little scared of such an approach. It seems to me we must have the courage to say not only that
there is a difference between A and B but what the difference is, what
A is doing and what B is doing. I go back to one of my favourite
quotations from Dell Hymes which goes something like this: 'It is
absurd to say that there could not have been one human culture until
there were two.'

Marie Clay I should like to bring up a point that Criper made about
the relatively static nature of the model and the importance of considering social change and conflict. In New Zealand we have some very
strong ethnic educational problems with the Maori indigenous population and various cultural groups coming from the Pacific Islands. The

critical question for us is how the child copes; I think sociolinguistic-ally we have passed the stage where we believe we were integrating these people into a standard culture. Instead we are looking to the coexistence of several cultures. My interest, therefore, as a develop-mental psychologist, is how the child acquires and adjusts to at least two social systems; and I am particularly interested in the question of the flexibility with which the child comes to handle multiple meanings in a variety of situations.

Halliday The approach that has sometimes come to be discussed under the heading of sociolinguistic competence or communicative competence, associated largely with Hymes, has had the effect of, perhaps, distracting attention away from the major issues. Essentially the child is not learning to behave in situations. We cannot explain what is happening in terms of a communicative competence defined as learning what language is appropriate. It is far too narrow a concept. The whole distinction between communicative competence and any other competence I find totally meaningless. The trouble has come from the misunderstanding by linguists of the whole notion of compe-tence. I suspect that Hymes has been attempting to exploit the interest in this term by building it into his own system but at a point where it does not really belong.

As to whether I have over- or under-valued language, I think the major issue at the moment is to see language in operation as an interpre-tation of something else before we are prepared to consider it as opera-ting independently as a determinant.

Bruner I think that what has emerged from this first part of the discus-sion is the sense that when one talks about a common field of meaning, or a semiotic of some sort, transmitting culture, one cannot narrowly conceive of it as being within just the framework of language. We are, in fact, coming to the notion of generalised sememes of the kind that Bar Hillel tried to talk about some years ago.

Bernstein It seems to me there are certain analytical problems in-volved in the discussion. The first is what really counts as the problem, because what counts as the problem also defines what counts as signifi-cant variation, what counts as the unit of analysis and the interrelation-ship between units. (In terms of Halliday's paper, I cannot see the connection between the institutional macro-relationship which he has outlined and the local relationships in terms of problems with which I myself am dealing.) The second problem is this: how does the child apply certain ground rules whereby he is able to generate and trans-form experiences, how does he reconcile the contention between different ground rules that are being transmitted in different socialised behaviours? If the question is put in this way—then we have conflict.

And therefore this is how I would put it: what range of options does the child have available to him in a regulative context? It might be possible to make use of Halliday's work on semantic choices in trying to answer this question.

Other points were made in the discussion by:
C. Fraser
A. Sloman
A. Davies

2

Dialect

H. H. SPEITEL

Central government and schools (controlled by central government) have, with few exceptions, seldom shown a tolerant or positive attitude to speech varieties loosely termed 'dialects'. In fact, for many the word dialect implies regionality, separateness, lack of communication, backwardness, ignorance, an inferior kind of speech, in short something diametrically opposed to the aims of a uniform basic education for all which forms the basis of a unified political body. Few countries have taken the seemingly straight course of condemning dialects through parliament as the French Assembly did in 1794[1] 'car ceux-ci sont le dernier anneau de la chaîne que la tyrannie vous avait imposée'. Dialect was here considered as a means of perpetuating inequality, and the cure lay in the introduction of instructors to be sent to every village to teach the French (standard) language and the meaning of the laws and decrees of the central government (written in Standard French). It is perhaps interesting to note that the decree did not have the desired effect but rather inspired a movement in defence of the patois.[2]

Even if one can see the point of view of governments, it is difficult to see the reasons for the neglect of dialects by linguists until quite recently. Especially in Great Britain the scientific study of dialects had to wait until the middle of the twentieth century to receive any large-scale academic attention (by the Survey of English Dialects in Leeds and the Linguistic Survey of Scotland (Scots and Gaelic sections) in Edinburgh). I am not forgetting a number of monographs on English and Scots dialects nor do I want to belittle the achievements of A. J. Ellis in his dialect survey at the end of the last century. I am referring more to the effects that the study of dialects should have had on the theoretical thinking of linguists working, say, in the field of historical linguistics. Nearly all of them chose (and some still choose) to ignore speech varieties and to base their studies exclusively on the examination of the standard language, because they find variety disturbing and difficult to fit into a pattern.

After these general critical remarks, let me turn to a specific language context which I know through first-hand experience, Lowland Scots, and examine a variety of problems (most of which have relevance to other language contexts) and then ask if a more positive attitude to these language varieties in schools may be a desirable goal.

One might often quickly reach agreement about whether a certain word or grammatical feature belongs to Standard English as spoken in Scotland (Scottish Standard English, henceforth referred to as SSE) or is definitely non-Standard and therefore slang or dialect or broad Scots or whatever term might be used.[3] Thus items like (1) *cod* [kod][4] 'pillow', *reek* [rik] 'smoke', *soutar* [sutər] 'shoemaker', that book is *mines* (my book), I'*se* warrant (I'll warrant), etc., will by many be called Scots dialect. There are however items like (2) I *doubt* that (think that), I was waiting *on* him, I got it *in* a present, *furth of, anent, uplift* v., *pinkie* (little finger), *maindoor flat*, etc., which are also used by people who would not use the first group of items and who would be recognised as SSE speakers (SSE = a regional variety of Standard English). Legal and administrative Scots accounts for a good deal of non-Southern English vocabulary (cf. (3) send the *missive, Depute* Town Clerk, *Sheriff Substitute, decreet arbitral, landward*, etc.) which is used as a matter of course by educated Scotsmen who would certainly reject examples (1) and some of (2) in their own speech or would be ignorant of (1).

Although the attribution of an item to one of the three groups proposed above might start (and usually does start) an argument with some people, some kind of agreement could probably be reached. This is not the case with the *pronunciation* of words. And yet it is the different pronunciation more than the vocabulary or grammar which accounts for what I want to call dialect. I am speaking here from my experience with the dialect in the Lothians, especially the urban areas, where the dialect vocabulary and dialectal grammatical features have almost disappeared. I found this confirmed when I tested dialect words which were elicited from old speakers on the younger generation. In most cases the latter were not able to supply me with a meaning of a word or were completely ignorant of its existence. Teachers working in an urban set-up are not very likely to come across dialect vocabulary like some of the items I listed above under (1). Some recognise items in (2) as Scots Standard and let them pass in speech but not in writing. When faced with pronunciations of words deviating from their own pattern considerably teachers often call them 'sloppy' or 'improper' although some display an astonishing degree of tolerance. On the whole corrections are eclectic and aimless.

I shall have to examine the phonology (sound system) of Scots in some detail in order to give an account of what I mean by SSE and dialect in pronunciation. For this purpose I have established rules based on personal research and work carried out by the Phonetics Department of Edinburgh University. Starting from the fact that there are many words which are shared by

Table

STRESSED VOWELS EXCEPT BEFORE '-r'

	RP No.	RP	SSE 1		SSE 2	SSE/dialect No.
beat	1	i ——	i ——————		i	1
bit	2	1 ——	1 ——————		1	2
bait	3	eɪ ——	e ——	e	E	3
bet	4	ɛ ——	ɛ ——	ɛ		
ham	5	a ——	a	a	A	4
balm	6	ɑ ——	ɑ			
caught	7	ɔ ——	ɔ	ɔ	O	5
cot	8	ɒ ——	ɒ	ɒ		
coat	9	oʊ ——	o ——	o		
hut	10	ʌ ——	ʌ ——————		ʌ	6
pool	11	u	u ——————		u	7
pull	12	ʊ				
tide	13	aɪ	ɛɪ		EI	8
tied			ae			
shout	14	aʊ ——	ʌu ——————		ʌu	9
boy	15	ɒɪ ——	ɔe ——————		ɔe	10

varieties of Standard English and the dialect, the so-called common core words (ccw), one can establish certain *regular* correspondences (*a*) between the sound systems of Southern English (which I give the cover name of RP (Received Pronunciation)[5] and SSE, and (*b*) between the sound systems of SSE and a number of Scottish dialects. The rather circuitous way of starting with RP was necessary because there does not exist up to the present day a pronouncing dictionary of SSE which lists forms acceptable to educated, non-dialect speakers of Scots. Such a work is urgently needed, especially for schools, but is rather difficult to produce, one of the problems being whether there is *one* standard and if not how many and which standards. In the table opposite I present an idealised form of SSE, i.e. SSE 1, a postulated form, a 'construct' which probably does not exist in many speakers but which fulfils a heuristic function whose importance will become apparent further on. I have tried to give a slightly fuller picture of it elsewhere,[6] here I can deal only with certain aspects. I stress again that to me it is a 'fiction' which needs much more experimental data to bring it nearer to 'reality'.

Only equivalent stressed vowels (except before '-r') in RP and SSE are shown. The *consonant* systems correspond to each other with minor exceptions and need not be considered here, except for one characteristic feature of SSE: most Scots people pronounce 'r' wherever it is written, i.e. in contrast to RP also after a vowel at the end of a syllable. Cf. the pronunciation of 'here, hair, harm' in RP [hɪə, hɛə, hɑm] and SSE [hir, her, harm].

We can transform an RP pronunciation of a ccw into SSE by following the lines connecting RP and SSE vowels and just leaving the consonantal symbols as they are.

Thus 'beat'   RP [bit]   SSE   [bit]
     'cheat' RP [ʧit]   SSE   [ʧit]
     'bit'   RP [bɪt]   SSE   [bɪt]
     'sit'   RP [sɪt]   SSE   [sɪt]

The symbols I use for the transcription should however not be considered to possess the same phonetic implications in both varieties[7] and this fact accounts for a good deal of the difference between them. E.g. RP vowel No. 2 [ɪ] is in most types of SSE a much opener vowel, phonetically [ɪ̞] or [ë] or [ɛ̈]. (To English ears some pronunciations of, say, 'big' [bëg, bɛ̈g] sound more like 'beg'.) There are, however, SSE speakers who use a sound very similar to RP [ɪ]. In some cases I have chosen a different symbol

in SSE 1 to draw attention to widely prevalent phonetic differences. Let us look e.g. at RP no. 3 [eɪ] and RP no. 9 [oʊ], SSE
[e] and [o] respectively. If one asks people to state differences in
pronunciation between RP and SSE, they will usually tell you
the Scots 'preserves the "pure" vowels', i.e. has monophthongs
[e] and [o]. This is correct for a great number of speakers, but
there are also quite a few who have an RP-like [ou], in fact I
believe in many educated speakers this feature is increasing. On
the other hand there are few Scots people who approach RP
[eɪ] although there is often a slight diphthongisation in open
syllable 'way [we¹], 'hay' [he¹].

I should like to draw attention to the three *boxes* under SSE 1.

(1) $\boxed{\begin{array}{c}a\\ɑ\end{array}}$: RP no. 5 and 6 often just have *one* SSE equivalent, a low

central vowel [ä]. If Scots people have two equivalents their distribution in ccw is usually different from RP: cf. e.g. 'bath' SSE
[baθ] vs. RP [bɑθ], 'gather' SSE [gaðər] vs. RP [gaðə] but the
choice of vowel often fluctuates in the same word in one and the same
speaker and certainly between speakers in a community. Children
and teachers sometimes clash in their distributions although in my
experience teachers usually do not bother to enforce their pronunciation in vowel areas which I have boxed. I notice however in
my own children that they have now started saying 'bath'
[baθ] and 'laugh' [laf] which they have not picked up from their

parents! (2) $\boxed{\begin{array}{c}ɔ\\ɒ\end{array}}$: for most Scots 'got' and 'caught' rhyme. If

children have the RP distinction this is often not noticed by

teachers. (3) $\boxed{\begin{array}{c}ɛ1\\ae\end{array}}$: this is a case where SSE has two vowels for one

in RP. Cases like 'tide' and 'tied' [tɛɪd—taed] 'side' and 'sighed'
[sɛɪd—saed] could be interpreted by having recourse to morphemic
criteria or juncture ([ae] before morphological boundary) and
one could then say that there is only one phoneme if complementary distribution for the other cases could be proved. But there
are sometimes minimal vowel distinctions in 'tire' v. and 'tyre'
n. and other cases. Although there are tendencies to have, say
[ɛɪ], mostly before plosives and [m, n, l, f, s] there is considerable
variation in one speaker and between different speakers of SSE.
In my experience Scottish teachers notice and correct deviations
in cases like 'tide' and 'tied' (but I have noted [tɛɪd] for 'tied' not

being spotted). For my purposes I have considered all fluctuations within boxes under SSE 1 as being regular SSE equivalents.

One of the most common differences in the vowel systems of RP and SSE is the merger of RP nos. 11 and 12 into one SSE vowel. For most SSE speakers 'pull' and 'pool' are perfect rhymes. There are however some who are close to the RP system and manage to keep the distinction in most cases, but one can nearly always discover slips and this merger is therefore one safe SSE marker. Thus 'moon' RP [mun] may appear as [mon] in some Scots speakers. The phonetic qualities of SSE [u] may also vary considerably from RP. In Edinburgh and elsewhere SSE [u] is often very centralised ([ü] or even more fronted) in all phonetic contexts. I have never noticed any corrections of pupils even at private schools which are thought to pride themselves on their English speech.

Turning now to the next column in the table (SSE 2), some further changes have been made. SSE 2 is a form of SSE which is closer to actual dialect (as defined below) speakers, whereas SSE 1 is more middle-of-the-road or tends towards RP. SSE 2 is at the same time an even more abstract entity and shows the minimal contrasts or the minimal system to be postulated for a number of, if not all, Scottish dialects.[8] I have replaced the boxes in SSE 1 by

symbols in capital letters, cf. A, EI. $\boxed{\begin{matrix} \text{ɔ} \\ \text{ɒ} \end{matrix}}$ can be replaced by [ɒ]

and this has been boxed with [o], i.e. subsumed under [O]. SSE [ɔ] derived from RP no. 7 is partly boxed with the merger of SSE 1 [a] and [ɑ] resulting in [A]. Some SSE [ɔ] go with [o] (cf. below) which in turn is boxed with [ɒ] resulting in [O] (note broken lines).

Before I sketch the phonetic implications let me say at once that I have not much acquaintance with this type of SSE at Edinburgh schools and that information on these items with regard to teachers' reactions would be welcome and valuable.

(1) E: SSE 1 [e] and [ɛ] have been subsumed because their phonetic realisations especially in dialect speakers fluctuate considerably within one person in the same word, and it is often difficult for this reason to attribute a certain speech sound within this group to one or the other 'pole'. Cf. the pronunciation of 'main' [men] (= SSE 1), [mẹn] (lowered [e]), [mẹn] (raised [ɛ]), [mɛn] or similarly 'place', 'race', etc.; 'breath' [brɛθ] (= SSE 1), [brɛθ], [brẹθ], [breθ] or similarly 'memory', 'very', 'heaven', etc. The fluctuation is particularly strong in dialect vocabulary where

there is not much pressure from SSE 1. Cf. *'baith'* (both), *'saip'* (soap), *'gless'* (glass), *'pairt/pert'* (part), etc.

(2) [O]: corresponding to [E] there is a great deal of fluctuation between [o] and [ɔ].

(*a*) cf. 'joke', 'bloke', 'hope', 'note', etc. with variants [o] (= SSE 1), [ǫ, ǫ̣, ɔ].

(*b*) 'rock', 'block', 'not', 'drop', etc. with variants ranging from [ɔ] (=SSE 1) to [o].

It is my impression that nowadays examples of (*a*) are more commonly heard in Edinburgh than (*b*), especially in the younger generation. I have been told by a Scot from Ayrshire that where in (*b*) the realisations reach [o], i.e. 'sock' and 'soak' fall together [sok], this would be corrected rather than if the two fell together in [sɔk].

Ccw which have RP no. 7 [ɔ] as e.g. 'hawk', 'sought', 'caught', 'taught', etc. are less likely to have the vowel raised to [o] in SSE 2 than those that have RP no. 8 [ɒ] except for those which have [w] in front of [ɔ], like 'war', 'warn', 'water'.

The way has now been cleared for my definition of dialect at the phonological level. I will return to the phonetic aspects once more later when I wish to discuss certain questions in relation to 'sloppy' speech.

To recapitulate: any ccw which shows regular correspondences and arrangement of consonants between RP and SSE and whose stressed vowels follow the correspondences along the lines suggested in the table with certain phonetic differences which can be specified and with possible variations subsumed in the boxes (or indicated by capital letters in the table) belongs to SSE. Any deviation in a ccw from this scheme I call a dialect form or a dialect pronunciation (= a distributional difference).

Examples	*SSE*	*Dialect*	*Code*[9]
both	boθ	bEθ	3.6
use v.	juz	jEz	3.7
point	pɔent	pEInt	8.10
about	əˈbʌut	əˈbut	7.9
full	ful	fu	CL(consonant loss)
path	paθ	pAd	CS(consonant substitution)

For most of these groups large numbers of words can be found.[10] In the Appendix I have listed the more important vocalic ones and have given examples for those groups which are still commonly encountered in Edinburgh, e.g. in the playground of most primary schools. Some of these groups will be found all over Scotland, others will be limited to certain areas of the country. My examples are all taken from the Lothians. Moving across to Fife would introduce new groups, some of the above would increase in numbers of ccw involved, others would disappear altogether or shrink. There are of course historical reasons for this, forces at work in the history of Scots and of English. But the synchronic comparison proposed here has the advantage that it does not only provide the dialect form but also states which form will appear in its place when the speaker changes from dialect to speaking SSE, an event which occurs very frequently in the Scottish linguistic context and which deserves some further consideration. The influence of Southern English (and, more recently, other regional varieties of Standard English) on the dialects might be considered of less importance in Scotland, but its impact on the shaping of SSE, especially in urban areas like Edinburgh, should not be underestimated. However, sometimes I feel that far too much is made of its (phonetic) influence through radio and television.

If we extend the meaning of *bilingualism* to include not only speakers of two different languages (e.g. Gaelic and English) but also of two different speech varieties like SSE and Scots dialect, we can say that most dialect speakers are nowadays bilingual. They are able to understand and more or less capable of speaking SSE[11]. The fact that the two speech varieties are closely related (belong to the 'same language'), e.g. share a large part of their vocabulary, the common core words (cf. above), accounts for a number of phenomena which I propose to consider now.

When a dialect speaker wishes or is forced to abandon his dialect, there are certain features which will disappear, features which he can consciously suppress or learn to suppress, features which he can control, so to speak. I have called them *primary dialect features*. At the phonological level they are mostly those which I have defined as dialect above.[12] But at the same time there will remain certain features in his SSE which he cannot abandon at will, over which he has less control, the so-called *secondary dialect features*. One such feature is the pronunciation of 'r' where it appears in writing after vowels as in 'here', 'there', 'farm', etc. As this 'r' persists in nearly all types of SSE, i.e. even in people who are not familiar with the dialect, its origin should be noted. Many phonetic features of SSE are ultimately derivable from secondary dialect features. Other important ones are intonation, rhythm, syllable division, etc. It would be wrong, however, to derive all phenomena in SSE which make it different from RP from their dialect origins, because in big urban communities at least, SSE develops new features which are due to other factors like social classes, social prestige, fashions, age groups, sex, etc. Of course rural dialects are subject to such forces as well, they change and have changed over the centuries, but this seems to have been less noticeable. (The present bilingual situation is conducive to changes in the dialect due to influence from SSE developments.[13])

Another problem arising from bilingualism is the question of 'pure' dialect. Any observer of Scottish dialect speakers may have noticed that with many of them it is not so much a question of their speaking *either* dialect *or* SSE but rather of *more* or *less* of the one variety or the other. People who can perform in 'pure' dialect consistently at all linguistic levels have become very rare. At the phonological level one and the same word may appear in the same stretch of speech, even in situations where 'maximal' dialect[14] could be expected,[15] sometimes in its dialect form and sometimes in its SSE form (e.g. [dʌun] and [dun] 'down' alternate or [fut] and [fɪt] 'foot' or the phrase 'It is well known'—'It's well kent', 'It's weel known', 'It's weel kent'). What makes the speaker a dialect speaker is his *potential* of producing an alternative for an SSE form. He has a *choice* of two (or more) pronunciations for many ccw,[16] a choice of a dialect lexical item as against a standard word, etc. The linguist has the task of sorting this mixture out which cannot be done without a certain degree of arbitrariness.

What implications do the preceding linguistic considerations have in a school context? I will keep to the phonological problems, but let me stress that I have no first-hand experience of dialect in the classroom.

Many children arrive at school with both varieties (SSE and dialect). This means that they must have picked up dialect forms in the first five years of their lives either from their parents or from older relatives (grandparents, aunts and uncles) or from early playmates. In a place like Edinburgh they have more often than not also learned at that age that, when faced with some kind of superior person who speaks English, one has to suppress dialect forms but that it is all right to perform in the dialect in a play situation. This is easily checked by listening to infants in the playground and in a classroom situation. Children who bring no dialect forms from their homes try to imitate their broadest-speaking classmates, pick up quite a number of dialect forms themselves and seem to be fascinated by them, as I have noticed in my own children's speech. Dialect forms carry a certain amount of prestige in the playground. How do these five-year-olds know, on the other hand, that dialect is not acceptable in the classroom? I suspect that (in Edinburgh at least) mothers admonish their children to speak 'proper' and reprimand their elders, as I have observed myself, for using dialect in front of the children. Girls seem to develop a stronger sense of what is 'proper'; at a later stage at school they will adopt more socially prestigious phonetic features of SSE (avoid glottal stops, use retroflexed 'r') or even take elocution lessons (a thing very rarely found with boys) and as mothers pass on their 'improvements' to their children. If we think of the large number of female primary school teachers we can well imagine why things are not going well for Scots dialect. Boys on the other hand seem to me to preserve and use the dialect more (as a sign of toughness, rebellion?). They use SSE for social reasons, but they do not seem to abandon their potential dialect forms willingly and gladly and as old men often return to a 'fuller' dialect. These are, of course, sweeping generalisations and would have to be tested thoroughly, but it is the impression we have gathered in the Linguistic Survey of Scotland in the course of our fieldwork. If girls/women do not develop an antipathy against dialect they often show a larger potential of dialect than their husbands and preserve a great deal of 'conservative' dialect forms. It is due to such 'resistant' types, both men and women, that the dialect has survived at all in urban communities in Scotland.

To return to schools. There are some children who are not able to distinguish between the two varieties (SSE and dialect) and use dialect forms in the classroom. I know of one such case in Edinburgh where a boy with a working-class background produced dialect forms in front of the teachers even after three years. He had several clashes with the teacher and did not do well in any subjects, but seemed to improve slightly with another temporary teacher. I had no chance to observe the child personally, he was eventually transferred to another school. There must be many like him. It would interest me very much to know if research has already been carried out on whether the inability to distinguish between language varieties in my sense hampers or restricts the ability to learn or is linked with a low IQ (quite apart from differences in 'code' attributable to social class). There seems to me a vast field of research here in Scotland.

Considering the importance of teachers' attitudes to dialect it would seem a worthwhile project to institute an enquiry about their opinions. Which 'mistakes' do they correct in speech, in reading, in writing, etc.? Have they any idea what the local dialect as spoken by adults sounds like? Do they think 'dialect' exists in the area where they are working? Who, do they think, speaks it? Is there in their opinion a place for the use of dialect at school or in Scotland at all? Did they speak dialect themselves at any time? (I have jotted down these questions in no particular order.)

I mentioned the vague terminology teachers apply to patterns different from their own. We have to keep in mind here that—unfortunately—most teachers have no linguistic training and many are not interested primarily in language. Loose terminology is of course not the prerogative of the teacher; even linguists (including myself) are sometimes guilty of this. From the point of view of somebody who is expected (or believes he is expected) to propagate a standard of pronunciation, or, seen from the angle of a historical dialectologist, some of the speech forms they meet are 'corrupted' or 'sloppy' or 'bad language'. Teachers who are concerned with teaching backward readers or drama teachers who want the children to use a pronunciation that is widely understood may often despair. Yet some of them were very astonished when I told them that certain features they were in particular concerned about were generally accepted (primary or secondary) dialect forms, which were probably used by the majority of speakers whom the children encountered. It seems to me, therefore, specially important for teachers of English to concern themselves with linguistics, and above all with phonetics, and to make it their task to listen to people, adults and children, carefully when they move to an area which is linguistically unfamiliar to them. Only then can they assess linguistically deviant forms they come across and decide if and how they may want to change them.

Let me give some random examples from Edinburgh.

(1) [ŋ] for SSE [ɪn] in kill*ing*, sing*ing*, danc*ing*, etc. is a dialect pronunciation which persists in many people's SSE (a secondary dialect feature).
(2) Similarly [ɪ, ë] for [o] in post-tonic syllables as in bar*row*, wind*ow*, arr*ow*, narr*ow*, etc. Less commonly found in SSE speakers than (1).
(3) [ɪ,ë] for SSE [ə] as in Goud*a*, Americ*a*, polk*a*, sod*a*, extr*a* is quite common.

(4) In some speakers [ʌ] and [ɒ] are very similar phonetically. If the teacher understands 'cup' as 'cop', 'duck' as 'dock' he should carefully check if these have actually fallen together in the speaker. Similarly 'work', 'bird' which only some Scots people pronounce with a central vowel ([wərk, bərd] will often appear as [wʌrk, bʌrd] which is understood as [wɔrk, bɔrd] by some teachers. Great leniency should be exercised in this vowel context (before 'r' + consonant(s)).

(5) Often [ʌ] and [a] sound very similar. In some phonetic contexts they are just distinguished by length in some speakers; cf. 'cap': 'cup' [kaːp] : [kap]. When the words are read out like this, some teachers may correct the pronunciation of 'cup'. If on the other hand [ʌ] and [a] fall together in [ʌ], as is relatively common in some phonetic contexts, this is often not noticed nor corrected: cf. 'branch', 'rash', 'banner' with [ʌ].

(6) RP [tʃ] in post-tonic syllables as in 'nature', 'creature', 'adventure', etc. has the regular SSE correspondence [tj], phonetically often [tj, tç]. Some Scots people insist on the pronunciation [tj̥, tç] being the only correct one. Similarly SSE [dj] for RP [dʒ] as in 'soldier'.

(7) The glottal stop [ʔ] as a variant of [t] in Edinburgh and elsewhere (and for other voiceless plosives as well, in other areas) in post-tonic position within a word[17] constitutes a particular headache for teachers, and the term 'sloppy' is often used in this context. Cf. 'water', 'bottle', 'city', 'batter', 'hat', 'hot' [wɔʔər, bɒʔl̩, sıʔı, baʔər, haʔ, hɒʔ]. It is thought to be an urban phenomenon, but is in fact encountered in remote villages in Scotland even with old people. Today the glottal stop in the above phonetic contexts is probably commoner than [t] in a great number of people in Edinburgh. Should we try to turn the clock back? This is a decision for the schools to make, not for the linguist. I personally do not think that such an attempt would be successful.

[ʔ] often also stands for [t] in post-tonic position after [l], [r], and [n] ('belted' [bɛlʔıd̥], 'auntie' [anʔı], 'quarter' [kwɔrʔər],) and less commonly perhaps in word-final position: 'belt' [bɛlʔ], 'tent' [tɛnʔ], 'quart' [kwɔrʔ]. With a good number of mostly working-class people, but also creeping into 'higher' strata [n] and [r] disappear before glottal stop in the disyllabic examples 'auntie' [aʔı], 'quarter' [kwɒʔər] and in some of the monosyllabic words like 'tent' [tɛʔ].

Where the [n] disappears nasalised vowels are sometimes used:
[tẽ˞], [wɔ̃˞ɪd̥] 'wanted'. A further step can be distinguished
where [ˀ] is weakened and disappears as in [wɔ(ˀ)ɪd̥], 'cut it'
[kʌ(ˀ)ɪˀ], etc. This may lead to great difficulties in understanding for teachers who are not familiar with this phenomenon and sometimes even for people accustomed to it.

These examples could be multiplied but might perhaps suffice
to illustrate the general problem. I was very pleased to see such
factors had been taken into account, probably for the first time in
Scotland, in assessing deviant speech forms in children in the
Edinburgh Articulation Test, Textbook, by A. Anthony *et al.*, Edinburgh 1971.

So far I have talked about dialect in an urban setting. What
about dialect at schools in more rural areas of Scotland? Especially
in the northern and north-eastern regions, dialect is still stronger
than in the industrial central belt. The reason for this situation is
that there has been far less *mobility* in the agricultural regions both
in a social and a geographical sense, and it is mobility perhaps
more than any educational force which has led to the disappearance of dialect.

Dialect in these peripheral areas means a variety which still
shows considerable differences in grammar and vocabulary from
SSE. At the phonological level we can expect to find (1) a large
number of groups of distributional differences like the ones shown
for Midlothian dialect [Ml] in the Appendix; (2) a large potential of
items in these groups; (3) more of these potential dialect forms to
appear more consistently in the speech of more people in a
greater variety of contexts than in Ml. Thus I have been assured
that infants arrive at school with a 'full' dialect and very little
awareness of SSE. There is now a group of headmasters and teachers interested in the problems that arise from this situation which
a hundred years ago must have been the rule rather than the
exception all over Scotland. Their work will give a chance to
observe the linguistic behaviour of these children and at the same
time to think again about the attitude teachers should adopt
towards Scots dialect.

This brings me to my final topic, namely the place of dialect
in Scotland and, implicitly, in Scottish schools. It may have been
noticed all along that I view the disappearance of dialect and the
rôle schools have played in this not altogether favourably. As a
linguist, I will, of course, try to avoid value judgements and there-

fore I have attempted not to take sides in many of the issues I touched on below. But at the same time I feel as a person involved in the study of dialects that with a little more care and thinking a better balance might have been achieved. I am pleading here for the coexistence of dialect and Scottish Standard English, whereas too often an either–or relationship has been set up between the two. In my opinion it is too late now for Scotland to try to imitate Switzerland (i.e. those areas of Switzerland where people speak a language variety derivable from Germanic), where nearly *everyone* speaks his own local dialect habitually when he is amongst Swiss people (including on occasions in parliament or local government or in schools) and where foreigners desiring to acquire Swiss nationality may in some areas be required to speak 'Schwyzertütsch'. German (*Hochdeutsch*) is used for communicating with Germans, on certain formal occasions in Switzerland, and in most types of writing (*Schriftdeutsch*)[18]. I have often heard a similar set-up being recommended for Scotland. However, local Scots dialects are *not* spoken habitually by the majority of Scotsmen and there is no question of a reform in Scotland in this field being possible by just everybody returning to Scots dialect.

The other solution proposed, e.g. by some members of the 'Lallans Society', namely to introduce a kind of 'synthetic' Scots as a new Scottish language, a Scots made up of Scottish dialect of all ages and all places, seems to me to promise even less success and I have warned against such an attempt.[19] 'Lallans' is inspired by people mostly interested in poetry and has therefore a rather limited range. It is true that the movement has inspired greater interest in Scots by its publications and I do not want to belittle its successes in any way, indeed, I find it strange that 'Lallans' has not received more attention by professional linguists. However, inventing a national language (i.e. 'distilling' a new kind of Scots from the Scots of all times and places) and succeeding in persuading people to accept this, are two entirely different matters. A 'national' language presupposes also that it will be used in serious prose writing and official communications (in this connection it could be asked if in this sense 'Schwyzertütsch' is a 'national' language). Yet, except for legal vocabulary, Scots has not preserved or developed its own linguistic vehicle for these purposes.

I feel that there is certainly a place for a wider use of SSE (even with a strong dialect flavouring, i.e. pronounced secondary dialect features) in Scottish public life and on radio and television —and at school. Other regional varieties of English, e.g. Midland

English, have established themselves in the media in recent years and public opinion seems to be in favour of it. At the same time it must not be overlooked that a strong Scottish (or English) accent is not easily understood, say, on the continent, where I expect young Scotsmen will be looking for jobs or commercial connections. After all, RP or American English is taught in almost all countries outside the Commonwealth, although SSE would be a much easier accent of English to teach and to learn, but that is a separate matter.

To return finally to dialect at school and the French revolution. There has certainly been a change in the interpretation of '*égalité*' in recent times. We speak of 'equal chances for all' not in the sense of imposing one standard everywhere but of trying to understand people of 'different' attitudes, behaviour patterns, social structures, etc., and by accommodating these in our society. People are rebelling against uniformity. Could not dialect in those areas where it is still a living speech form benefit from this tendency? Could people not be educated to understand their dialect as a distinct speech form with its own history and its own value,[20] worthy to exist beside Standard English? Schools could and should play their part in this although they have only just started thinking about the problem.[21]

Appendix

Distributional Differences of Stressed Vowels in ccw between SSE and Ml Dialect

In the following list I have ordered groups of ccw with distributional differences (cf. p. 40) in order of size (col. 1) for Ml dialect. The *code* refers to the last column in the Table (cf. p. 36), SSE/dialect no. Thus 3.4 means that words with a stressed SSE vowel 3 [E] appear in Ml dialect with vowel 4 [A]. The next column [Ml total] gives the total number of words found in each group in Ml (regardless of place or person]. Column E* total provides the comparable figure for a middle-aged Edinburgh speaker and the last column [E*] shows the order of size of groups in E*.

I have given examples for those groups which seem to me to be still in existence in urban Edinburgh.

Ml	Code	SSE →dialect	Ml total	E* total	E*
1	3.4	A → E	287	87	1
2	1.2	1 → i	211	43	3
3	1.3	E → i	107	41	4
4	7.9	ʌu → u	97	46	2
5	2.5	ʌ → 1	93	11	9
6	3.1	i → E	82	5	13
7	2.7	u → 1	75	13	7
8	4.3	E → A	61	4	—
9	4.6	O → A	58	10	10
10	9.6	O → ʌu	54	9	11
11	2.3	E → 1	51	18	5
12	3.6	O → E	49	17	6
13	1.8	EI → i	47	12	8
14	7.5	ʌ → u	42	6	12
15	3.7	u → E	40	9	11
16	8.10	ɔe → EI	31	12	8
	5.2	1 → ʌ	31	4	—
17	7.6	O → u	30	5	13
18	2.8	EI → 1	26	4	—
19	2.4	A → 1	24	3	—
20	8.3	E → EI	22	6	12
21	5.7	u → ʌ	19	6	12
22	6.5	ʌ → O	18	2	—
23	5.4	A → ʌ	16	1	—
24	3.2	1 → E	15	2	—
25	5.6	O → ʌ	14	3	—
26	5.9	ʌu → ʌ	13	2	—
27	9.7	u → ʌu	12	1	—
28	2.1	i → 1	9	1	—
	5.3	E → ʌ	9	1	—
	9.4	A → ʌu	9	—	—
	9.5	ʌ → ʌu	9	1	—
29	2.11	3 → 1	8	—	—
30	1.7	a → i	7	1	—
	3.8	EI → E	7	—	—
31	2.6	O → 1	6	—	—
	6.3	E → O	6	3	—
	6.2	1 → EI	6	—	—
32	1.4	A → i	5	—	—
	7.2	1 → u	5	1	—

Examples

3.4   Aberdeen, broad, glad, imagine, apple, cap, matter, natural, Saturday, axe, jacket, sack, family, manner, travel, father, gather, rather, after, grass, master, plaster, national, arm, army, arse, carry, charge, charity, clerk, farm, garden, yard, guard, harm, heart, march, narrow, party, smart, start, etc.

1.2   nigger, signature, drip, typical, pity, sick, finish, minute, opinion, pinafore, pin, sieve, his, visit, decision, vision, competition, malicious, superstition, vicious, etc.

1.3   neighbour, bread, dead, dread, head, lead, spread, steady, stretch, lemon, friend, meant, devil, eleven, seven, blaze, pleasant, deaf, breast, jelly, well adv., pear, swear, tear, wear, weigh.

7.9   about, doubt, shout, stout, brown, count, crown, down, gown, round, sound, town, mouth, south, house, mouse, coward, flower, hour, shower, sour, cow, how, etc.

2.5   but, flutter, done, one, other, does, dozen, just

1.8   oblige, spider, china, semolina, crisis, liar, eye, fly, lie

2.3   red, yet, engine, pencil, twenty, present, measure

2.7   foot, good, should, brute, fruit, put, soot, afternoon, spoon, use n.

3.6   home, comb, alone, stone, own, clothes, both, most, whole, floor, more, sore, so, toe

3.7   use v., whose, usual, poor, sure, do, shoe, too, who

4.6   drop, top, blow, crow, row n.

8.10   join, point, choice, boil, oil, spoil

9.6   grown pp., grow, soul, four, row v.

7.5   double, duck v., stucco, suck, sucker

7.6   pour, court n.v., bowl v., bowls n.pl.

NOTES

1. Cf. Pop, S., *La Dialectologie*, Louvain [1950], vol. 1, pp. 11f. The decision of the Assembly was based on a report by curé Gregoire with the title 'Rapport sur la nécessité de détruire les patois'.
2. Dialects have been much tougher at surviving than politicians and, indeed, linguists have thought, although the number of dialect speakers has declined.

3. SSE is usually referred to by dialect speakers as 'just the English'. I cannot here attempt to define slang v. dialect, but would rather draw the attention to the fact that 'slang' is popularly often used for the phenomena I shall deal with below.

4. I use IPA symbols in square brackets in my transcription which does not claim to be strictly phonemic.

5. I.e. those standard varieties which share identical (or almost identical) numbers and arrangement of phonemes with that variety commonly called RP and described in the works of Daniel Jones, although their *phonetic* realisation may differ considerably from RP and from each other. Cf. Jones, D., *Everyman's English Pronouncing Dictionary*, 12th ed., Dent, London 1963.

6. Speitel, H. H., *Some Studies in the Dialect of Midlothian*, Ph.D. thesis, Edinburgh 1969.

7. The RP symbols are phonemic contrasts. SSE 1 and SSE 2 symbols denote 'minimal' contrasts. SSE 1 symbols imply varying degrees of *similarity* with RP, but one might as well use abstract symbols as I have done for SSE 2.

8. Again, further research is required to substantiate this claim.

9. The figures refer to the right-hand column in the table on p. 36. (SSE/dialect no.). The first digit (3) refers to the dialect vowel [E], the second digit (6) to the SSE vowel which it has replaced [O]. In the Appendix the same information has also been stated in the form O→E, i.e. in the dialect form SSE [O] has been 'changed' to [E].

10. Cf. my thesis (fn. 6) for full exemplification.

11. Many SSE speakers in Scotland are not bilingual in this sense.

12. Dialect features like [rund], [dun], [fit] for 'round, down, foot' will disappear and be replaced by SSE [ʌu] and [u], but the phonetic quality of these SSE vowels will remain the same as where they occur in dialect vocabulary, say, in *nowt* 'cattle' [nʌut] or *loonie* 'imbecile' [lunɪ].

13. Features in some Lothian dialects which *might* be due to SSE developments include flapped or retroflexed 'r' [r,ɻ] for the trill [r], glottal stops [ʔ] in certain positions for [t], a more centralised [ü] for [u], etc.

14. As many dialect forms at all levels as possible.

15. Such a favourable situation would exist where the speaker is talking to members of the same family or persons of the same speech community about, say, an emotional topic, like a death or an accident.

16. It should be noted that a great number of ccw have no 'dialect' alternative as defined by me but if used by a dialect speaker can appear only in their regular form (cf. words like 'nice', 'happy', take' (in the Lothians the form [tak] is extinct), etc.

17. Little is known about the distribution of glottal stops in groups or

clauses and there seems, e.g. to be a restriction for some speakers on how many they can use in succession.

18. For a good short description in English, cf. Keller, R. E., *German Dialects*, Manchester 1961, pp. 30ff.

19. This leads often to rather obscure words being resurrected and used like '*kyngric*' for kingdom, '*leid*' for language or new inventions like '*leeddarger*' (lead-worker) for plumber.

20. It is not easy to pinpoint this value. There is a lot of emotion and sentiment about dialect which need not necessarily be a bad thing. As I have said before dialect has been a changing and living phenomenon and it is no use decrying every *change* as a corruption, but the *disappearance* of dialect in the central belt over the last fifty years is quite alarming. By encouraging projects on dialect, by pointing out dialect forms at an early stage at school and explaining about their *history*, in short, by showing *tolerance* and understanding, a sense of value which is more based on observation and fact might be developed in children and adults.

21. Cf. Low, J. T., 'Scottish Literature in the Schools' in *Scottish Literary News*, vol. 1, nos. 3 and 4, 1971, pp. 66–81. The Association for Scottish Literary Studies, who edit *SLN*, is also concerned with the study of Scots language with special reference to its place in schools.

What I call dialect is a kind of fiction. But I thought that with the aid of the table on page 36 of my paper one could work out certain things and make some value judgements about what pupils actually say in the classroom. When I wrote this paper I was not aware that three papers on the subject have recently appeared in Germany. I think it is worth mentioning some of the points in those papers.

1. One of the authors (Hasselberg) classifies children by parents' occupation; if parents have a mixed background he takes the higher status to classify the child. This seems to me nonsense because, as I suggest in my paper, in the West women—mothers and women teachers —have a much greater influence than men in changing children's speech habits.

2. The solution I offer, namely that of preservation, tolerating both the dialect and Standard Scottish English (SSE), has become less obvious to me since reading these German works where it is argued that children who are dialect speakers have genuine difficulties at school in all subjects. If this is indeed the case (and I would welcome your opinions on the situation here) then we must rethink our toleration solution.

3. One of the German writers suggests that dialect speakers benefit from studying other languages in school such as Latin. He also points out that many dialect-speaking parents prefer to see their children

studying scientific subjects which are more likely to be remunerative. I should be interested in your opinions on parental choices of this kind. May I now say a little about the table on page 36. My model proposes that whenever you can transform a lexical item that is shared by SSE and the dialect according to the lines connecting the sounds in the table, then these are *standard* forms. That means that there are common core words in SSE and the dialect. What I call dialect then is the distributional difference in the vowels which appears in the column headed SSE 2. So if for *soap*, for which the regular SSE pronunciation is [sop] somebody says [sep] then he would use a sound or group of sounds which I indicate by capital E, and I should call that a dialect pronunciation. This is all based on observation in schools. I did a little work on speech variation in Edinburgh schools some ten years ago. What it showed me was that there is a coherent SSE; certain pronunciations are accepted, others are always pounced on and corrected. These are the ones I have called dialect.

The questions I want to raise here are these. If a forceful attempt is made to change the phonological pattern of monoglot dialect speakers in primary schools, does this do harm to children? Again, if a child is not able to switch over in the common core words from one variety to the other, is this indicative of other things, say lower intelligence or adjustment difficulties? Is there any value in giving clear directions to teachers as to which dialect pronunciations they should accept and which reject? When I was a boy at school in Germany my dialect was being corrected constantly towards High German, thus my *Tach* was always corrected to *Tag*. I am told now that in certain parts of Germany this has changed and teachers are given more latitude—but still an explicit kind of latitude. Would that be of any use here?

NOTES

1. U. Ammon, 'Dialekt als sprachliche Barriere. Eine Pilotstudie über Schwierigkeiten von Dialektsprechern im Schulaufsatz', in *Muttersprache* **82** (1972), pp. 224–237.
2. J. Hasselberg, 'Die Abhängigkeit des Schulerfolgs vom Einfluss des Dialektes', in *Muttersprache* **82** (1972), pp. 201–223.
3. H. Löffler, Mundart als Sprachbarriere', in *Wirkendes Wort* **22** (1972), pp. 23–39.

Discussant: *Gillian Brown*

Hans Speitel's paper performs a valuable service in drawing a number of principled distinctions along a dialect scale which moves from RP through a notional SSE (Standard Scottish English) to a notional urban Scottish dialect. I shall rely upon the distinction that he draws, between the 'acceptable' dialect of SSE and the 'less acceptable' representative urban dialect, to ask several very specific questions which seem to me to represent the sorts of social and educational problems which arise when two dialects confront each other. The situation I have chosen to talk about is the situation in the primary school where the teacher speaks SSE and the child speaks a local Scottish dialect.

A striking confrontation of the standard form and the dialect form comes early in the child's education when he begins to learn to read. One interesting question here is: when the teacher draws the child's attention to the relationships holding between the phonological system and the orthographic conventions, does she concentrate on the relationship between the orthographic conventions and her own phonological system or on the relationship between the orthographic conventions and the phonological system of the child? Does the child have to learn the teacher's pronunciation of the word 'home' in order to establish a relationship between orthographic *o* + 'magic *e*' and his own pronunciation, 'hame'? Does this constitute a difficulty for the child?

A further set of questions may be asked about the child's ability to identify words which he has heard only in normal familiar speech, with the slow, clearly enunciated forms which the teacher produces in the reading situation. Consider the phrase 'going to'. In his everyday life the child may have heard many phonetically different performances of this phrase—[gʌnʌ], [gɔne], [goʌne], [goɪnte], etc. Does the child identify the slow, fully stressed forms pronounced by the teacher with this familiar phrase? Is it generally true that the child will find it hard to identify grammatical forms which normally turn up in speech as unstressed and phonetically closely bound to lexical items, like the 'to' in 'going to', with discrete stretches of print, bounded by spaces, which the teacher in order to pronounce at all has to stress in a way which is very rare in normal speech? This problem, if indeed it is a problem, is not confined to situations where differences of dialect are involved, but we may reasonably suppose that it will be more acute in these situations.

Speitel raises the question which confronts the teacher in the cross-dialect situation who has a pupil whom, she judges, people in the world at large will find difficult to understand because of the density of local forms in his speech. Should she try to modify the child's speech habits and, if so, how can she do this without threatening the child's own image of himself and of his relation to his home background? What are the features she should concentrate on? She might attempt to modify the primary dialect features that Speitel describes—the noticeably dialectal vowel qualities and the intervocalic glottal stop—or she might simply correct the pronunciation of the occasional word which happened to strike her as deviant. Speitel's paper suggests that random correction can frequently be observed. One would guess that random correction would have little general effect on the phonological feature that the teacher is trying to modify. We should notice Speitel's observation that most children by the age of ten have managed to become bilingual as between SSE and their own dialect. If this process is achieved without overt correction by the teacher it may well be advisable for the teacher to refrain from comment on the child's pronunciation.

I should like to turn now to an area which is briefly mentioned by Speitel, and that is the area of phonological suprasegmentals— rhythm and intonation—and those variables which we may call 'paralinguistic' features like loudness, the placing of the intonation contour higher or lower in the individual's pitch range and what I shall loosely term 'voice quality'. As Speitel suggests, the suprasegmental features of one dialect may differ in some respects from those of another dialect. Similarly paralinguistic features may vary between dialects. I would hazard a guess that we all share a similar way of expressing sincerity. We all tend to sink down in our voice ranges and speak, as it were, from the heart. In speaking confidentially we may 'lower our voices' both in pitch and amplitude. These may be features common to all English dialects. But I think there are modes of expression which differ from one dialect to another. Several primary school teachers have reported to me that children from socially deprived areas often do not understand that a command is a command unless it is marked as a command in a very obvious manner—marked, for example, by loud-ness or by 'steely voice' or by some other propelling of the personality of the person giving the order on to the child intended to receive it. And, they say, the child does not interpret this as a mark of any special attitude on the part of the teacher—it is simply the mark of an order that is to be obeyed. On the other hand we may suspect that a child from a different background would react to an order marked in this way as suggesting anger or impatience on the part of the speaker. He may well react with fear and dislike of this teacher who shouts at him unnecessarily. Similarly the teacher will have notions of what is the appropriate sound level in a given situation. She may commend a child who speaks loudly and clearly when he is at some distance from her but if he maintains this level when he comes close to her (since he is used to speaking loudly in this situation at home) the teacher may complain that the child is aggressive or rude. It is important that the child should learn, and that the teacher should learn, what sorts of paralinguistic variables are acceptable in different social situations in different dialect situations.

The ability to control the suprasegmental and paralinguistic features of the standard language will also affect the child's success in those school activities which involve reading aloud—activities like Burns' poetry reading competitions, Christmas plays and prepared speeches in class debates. In these activities the teacher tends to commend the child who reads 'with expression'. I asked a group of primary school children if they knew what this phrase means. They agreed that it means not only pausing at punctuation marks, speaking, as it were, in meaning-ful syntactic chunks, but, as one child nicely put it, 'acting with the voice'—speaking in a quavery old man's voice when an old man is supposed to be speaking, and speaking in a long-drawn-out whisper to indicate eerie suspense. They also said that there were some children who read very fast and fluently, pausing at the right places and making syntactic sense, who did not read 'with expression' in this sense. We may wonder why it is that some children appear to be able to master reading coherently but fail to progress to reading interestingly. It may be of course that they are simply not interested in what they are reading or it may be that they lack the self-confidence or the desire to express emotion in front of an audience. But we may wonder if it is sometimes because they are not familiar with the notion of putting oneself in somebody else's position, of speaking with his voice and seriously trying to interpret his emotion, in a reading situation. If reading aloud is an activity which is associated only with the use of the standard language in school it may be that these children need to be explicitly taught the suprasegmental and paralinguistic conventions whereby emotion can be expressed in this situation. The most appropriate time to do this may be in drama classes.

The ability to control appropriate suprasegmental and paralinguistic cues may be more important than the ability to control acceptable segmental cues in most situations in school and in everyday life. A statement spoken with a perfectly polite intention may sound bullying and assertive in the mouth of someone who does not know what the cues are which mark politeness in a given dialect situation. Suprasegmental and paralinguistic cues colour very strongly the effect of the verbal message. We can, I think, hardly overestimate the importance of research into this neglected area of dialect variation—neglected, I suspect, because its investigation awaits the arrival of a coherent theory of the identification and function of paralinguistic variables. Any research into the effect of dialect variation on interpersonal interaction in the classroom cannot afford to ignore this neglected area.

I have raised questions in four main areas. The first is the question of whether the teacher relates orthographic conventions to her own phonological system rather than to that of the child, and, if she does, whether this constitutes a hindrance in the process of learning to read. (A related question is, is this the child's formal introduction to the phonological system of the standard form of the language?) The second question is whether the child readily relates the citation forms of isolated words produced by the teacher to the forms he is already familiar with, especially when these forms are grammatical items which are normally unstressed and rarely occur in isolation. The third is the question of the value or propriety of attempting to modify the child's pronunciation. The last question concerns the possible differences in the use of suprasegmental and paralinguistic features in different dialect situations, and the way these differences may modify the child's view of the teacher and the teacher's view of the child.

GENERAL DISCUSSION

Gatherer There has been a change in official policy since the 1940s. Then it was possible for government reports on education in Scotland to speak of the 'speech of the streets' and the 'unremitting struggle against the dialect', etc. Recent reports refer to the need for the modern teacher to see language as an important part of social activity, the need for teachers to look at language as it is spoken rather than to try to impose new linguistic habits on children.

We cannot avoid sociolinguistic complexity in any discussion of the relationship between dialect and education. We do not know whether certain Scottish children are hampered in education by their dialect or by having a working-class background, or both. I think the work which R. S. K. Macaulay is just beginning, looking at the attitudes of dialect speakers in Glasgow and trying to relate these to educational aspirations, is crucial here. And so of the questions raised by Brown the most interesting to me is the one concerned with teachers' attitudes towards the linguistic environment of the classroom.

Jessie Reid I agree with Brown that the acquisition of literacy by the dialect speaker is a crucial issue. One can ask whether it is possible for the child to learn to read in dialect or whether he must do so in SSE. This relates to the amount of bidialectism in the home. This is a related problem which interests me. Is it possible, in fact, to present primary reading texts in dialect? But there are problems: should *home* be written *haim, hame,* or *haem*? If the child learns to respond with *hame* to *home* and he then reads the word *home* he will not want to say *hame* because to him they are not equivalent. Additional irregularities would be created on top of the existing spelling irregularities.

I think the crucial issues are: can the child become bilingual and can he accept switching? There may be a few limited cases where you can accept a dialect response to a standard written form—e.g. the Cockney [v] for the voiced [ð] in words like *mother*. But even here the child has to learn that this is not how you spell a [v] sound.

Speitel Whenever I have put a box in the SSE 1 column in my table I am suggesting there is no need for teachers to insist on a phonetic distinction. I am talking in phonological terms. What seems to me wrong is that teachers do insist on distinctions between, for example, *caught* and *cot* even though 90% of their children make no such distinction and never will. Teachers, in fact, need instruction in language and especially in phonology.

Bernstein I think it only fair to ask you to respond more specifically to the four questions raised by Brown. These were, if I may remind you: (1) whose system should be taken as critical in relating the written form to the spoken, teachers' or pupils'; (2) the discontinuity between citation form and regular speech forms; (3) the problem of corrections; and (4) the use of suprasegmental or paralinguistic features in the classroom situation.

Speitel Let me answer these in turn. (1) I have no experience that is relevant to this question. (2) On the whole I find that Scottish teachers let things like *goan tae* or *gun tae* or, say, *gonnae* pass and they do not correct them. Indeed, many teachers in Scotland use one of these forms in their own speech and are unaware of it. If a teacher from England comes in and says *going to*, I think the children listen to this and just go on saying *gonnae*, etc. Most teachers in my experience do not interfere, and I think they are right. (3) I am against *random* corrections. I think people should make up their minds whether they want Scottish dialect to continue to exist or not. But I think we need research on whether dialect speakers are at a disadvantage educationally. (4) I agree with Brown about the suprasegmental features. There are differences between Scottish and English usage here. I would add 'whining' to Brown's example of shouting. I have been told that there are many children in Edinburgh schools who do this all the time, talking normally.

Criper It seems to me that Brown's aim is to ask questions which the teachers here would in fact pick on and say 'Yes, these are the specific kinds of questions the answers to which, if one can find them, will be useful for language-teaching policy, teacher-training policy, or the like.'

Margaret Clark May I take up the question of oral reading by the child who is already a fluent reader. Since dialect differences are most marked in *written* words, if the child with the strong dialect is being presented with individual words to read aloud this may be putting an additional barrier to such a child in the learning-to-read situation. This could be measured and could be relevant educationally.

Joan Tough I agree this may be a critical problem for some children, but surely not for the majority. There is evidence that children can cope with inconsistencies. After all even in Scotland children presumably understand television which transmits much of the time in some kind of English English. There seems to me a problem, though, for children who can understand but who cannot make themselves understood.

Speitel As a problem it exists for few, those children from a dialect background who have reading difficulties. Their teachers do not know whether their problems are dialect or psychological problems.

Halliday As well as suggestions for academic research I hope we shall pay attention to other kinds of useful activity. For example, I think there is a vast area of exciting possibilities for teachers and pupils in what one might call the *exploration* of language, once the energies and natural curiosity of the teachers and children have been released. I would instance the language diary notion—a fascinating tool for a kind of practical research. I would hope that we might at least raise a number of headings under this general concept.

Bruner The suprasegmental question raised by Brown seems to me dossibly to relate to social relationships. If this is so, if the use of these features is to be interpreted as an invitation to participate in particular social relationships, then it might be valuable to get children to play out what it is they expect from a speaker who uses a heavily dialectic intonation.

Sinclair I have another question. Do children in Scottish schools ever express the wish for a form of speech that they do not possess? Or does the impulse to do something about the dialect stem from the teacher and the system?

Jessie Reid I have heard children express a desire *not* to acquire standard speech, expressed very, very forcibly: 'Please, miss, we dinna want to talk pan loaf.'

Davies Is there a problem of lack of intelligibility in Scottish schools between teacher and pupils? As I read Speitel's table (p. 36), because there are fewer vowels in SSE 2 there are likely to be more words that are the same.

Speitel No, my construct does not suggest there is likely to be a problem of intelligibility.

Britton I do not care for the idea of 'correction'. I think we need to put a *positive* value on the home speech of a child, and therefore anything we do in school should be adding to it and not correcting it. I am perfectly clear myself as to what is wanted in terms of the relation between the dialect and the written language—which I take to be the heart of the matter.

Many of the problems with regard to variation between dialect and standard forms can be left to settle themselves, I reckon, when the child faces the necessity of dealing with the written language. I agree with Brown that we do need to change teachers' attitudes towards language —there was a nice piece of low-level research by Johnson in New York in which he observed teachers over a period of time, tape-recording them, and then found a delightful correlation between the forms they were correcting on one occasion and exhibiting on another.

Bernstein This has, I think, been a very useful session because of the specification of research areas by Speitel and Brown. May I add two other questions? (1) what is the range of speech that the child can understand and under what conditions? I know lots of children who speak a non-standard English but who are incredibly capable of mimicking all kinds of pop songs. (2) To what extent is the child's experience outside the school validated by the interactions within the school—to be more precise, by the framework which the pacing of knowledge imposes on the teacher. The question of dialect raises a number of fundamental issues.

Other points were made in the discussion by:
  I. Morris
  H. Widdowson
  C. L. Boyle

3

Language as an Instrument of Thought

J. S. BRUNER

There has, of course, been a vast amount of literature on the relation of language and other manifestations of mind, mostly concerned with the question of how language affects the mental processes. Interest has centred particularly on the manner in which language shaped thought, though research on language-induced selectivity in perception has been almost as popular. In the era when cultural relativity was a dominant theme, it was hoped that one could find a *Weltanschauung* contained in each particular language that would give a unique cultural cast to the thought of members of that linguistic community. Today the emphasis has shifted more toward language (and cultural) universals and how, in general, they impart a universally human character to all information processing, whatever the culture. The concept of the psychic unity of mankind has replaced the doctrine of cultural relativism.

Modern structural linguistics, searching for universal deep structures in all languages, has contributed to this latter trend. One begins with certain ubiquitous features of grammar. Psycholinguistic research then seeks to explore the 'psychological reality' of grammar generally and of the underlying structure of sentences in particular. Does grammar provide a description not only of language as a corpus, but of the way in which a user 'competent' in the language generates sentences and, perhaps, processes the 'reality' encoded in the sentences? If it is assumed (as it was, but is no longer) that sentences are made up of a kernel string in the declarative mode, to which are added P (passive), Q (query), or N (negative) transformations, will this grammatical rule show up in information processing? Would a subject more likely retain 'knowledge' embodied in the kernel string while forgetting the information embodied in optional transformations performed on the string: e.g., for the sentence, *Was the boy not bitten by the dog?* would the subject be more likely to forget the N, P, and Q transformations and end up retaining only *The dog bit the boy*, the more durable kernel?

It is interesting that so much of the emphasis in research past and present has been one-directional: the influence of language on one or another of the cognitive processes. The reasons, historical and substantive, seem evident enough. The humanist tradition has always concerned itself with what it is that is most uniquely human about human mental life—and surely man's status as a language user is first in the list. One would then properly study the impact of language on other manifestations of human life, including thought. Cultural relativism, as noted, provided yet another one-way emphasis; and so too its ideological embodiment represented by the social definition of reality in Marxist epistemology that led Russian investigators to work so hard on the Pavlovian Second Signal System. Probably the anti-mentalism of much of psychology also inhibited traffic in the other direction: studies of the influence of mental processes on the nature of language when mental processes were being revised! In any case, there has been surprisingly little research done on many obvious problems of the relation of thought and language outside the range of the general debate about whether or not and in what ways language affected thought—the Whorf–Sapir–Humboldt issue. There has been little until recently on language as a tool or instrument of thought or problem solving, on how limitations in information processing impose constraints on language using, or on 'language-thought' compatibilities and incompatibilities and on the kinds of problems whose solutions are aided or hurt by language use. Even with respect to how cognitive processes shape language, a natural topic, it has been rare to find examples like the one that sought to explain the limit on sentence embedding ('This is the dog that the cat that the rat . . .') by reference to our limited memory. No matter that it was incorrect: it is a decidedly non-trivial idea. There is surely much to be gained from such inquiries into psychological constraints on languages. For an appreciation of such constraints can also tell much about how language may aid in transcending these limits, much as a microscope bypasses the resolving limit of the visual system and a computer the simultaneous processing limits of mental reckoning. The studies of the organisation of action by linguistic means, carried out with children in the Soviet Union (e.g., Martsignovskaya [1961], and Abramyan [1958]) are an example, albeit simple, of this line of work.

And what happens to one who *uses* the tools of language, not directly from the possession of language itself, but from sheer use of it as a tool kit? What happens to the mind of a creature who spends a great deal of his most effective waking time withdrawing attention from the non-verbal environment and *paying very close attention indeed* to the major properties of speech flow in which grammatical changes are signalled: word order, composition, affixation, internal modification, reduplication, accentual modification, segmentation, marking, and the rest? Will he not be profoundly different from one whose attention has been directed principally to non-linguistic perceptions—figures on grounds, groupings, gradients, etc? And more particularly, does it matter that one *writes* and *reads* rather than *talks* and *listens*; compresses one's message into the form of mathematics and formal logic, or uses only 'natural languages'; paraphrases the message for somebody else rather than simply receiving and 'noting' it?

You will see, I think, that my bias in approaching the psychology of language and thought is that of instrumentalism, and I would like to explain why. The first and most obvious reason is that I believe that it is a fruitful area of research as well as a neglected one. In the threefold division of linguistics into syntactics, semantics, and pragmatics proposed by Morris [1938] a generation ago, it is the last that has received the least attention, though it is most naturally suited to the research operations of the psychologist. Secondly, as a student of human development I am struck (as was Vygotsky [1962]) by the enormous importance of linguistic techniques for 'organising our thoughts about things', to use John Dewey's celebrated phrase. In the same vein, I must report that in my own research and that of my collaborators, e.g., Bruner, Olver and Greenfield [1966]) schooling appears to have a profound effect on a large number of mental processes, and I am rather convinced that the chief effect of schooling is to cultivate during development the use of language outside the context of action—a matter with which we shall be concerned later. And finally, there is by now a sufficient corpus of work on the impact of poverty and social helplessness on mental functioning to suggest that the use of language as an instrument is implicated, and I need only cite the work of our Chairman (Bernstein [1961]) and the work in sociolinguistics that it has sparked.

So I shall concentrate upon some crucial ways in which language is an instrument of thought and explore some of the educational implications of the inquiry.

II

Before turning to the matter at hand, we do well to sweep up some of the debris of past debates. A recent paper of George Miller's [1973] provides some good opening. He begins by asking:

> Once upon a time 'the growth of vocabulary' was an active field of research in American psychology, but in recent years little has been written about it. What happened? Were all our questions answered so that further work became unnecessary? Or is vocabulary growth a problem temporarily neglected, but soon to be discovered? Or is it possible that studies of vocabulary growth did not dry up, but that the old questions were re-formulated in a new way under a different name? A case can be made for each explanation. But, it is not obvious that any service would be rendered by deciding among them . . .

Miller then explores the changes in fashion of the last quarter century, changes that have, I think, affected our ways of looking at the relation between language and cognition.

During 'Phase I' the typical study of vocabulary growth attempted to estimate the number of words a child controlled, and then correlated his mastery with IQ or school grades (both rather high, with Templin [1957] showing that more than a third of the variance in the Stanford–Binet could be accounted for by this one factor and Cazden [1971] arguing for its centrality as an indicator of the child's mastery of distinctions in the world around him). The underlying model of language, among psychologists of this early period, was associationistic, and the amount of vocabulary was for them as good a reflection as any of the web of linguistic associations the child had mastered. But there was not much to say after one had noted, as Smith [1941] had, that the recognition vocabulary of the average eight-year-old increased at about the rate of 29 words (or 16 phonemes) per day.

As Miller remarks, 'While vocabulary was becoming unfashionable, grammar was becoming all the rage. Young psychologists who in earlier decades might have studied the acquisition of vocabulary were now captivated by the arcane intricacies of grammar acquisition'. Phase II was ushered in. The associationist metaphor of Phase I could be seen in all its inadequacy once one pondered the intricacy of grammar that made 'blind Venetians' not at all suggestive of 'Venetian blinds' and kept last words in sentences from being associated with the first ones in the sentences following. Nor could the little words, the *bys*, *ands*, *buts*, and

ifs, be treated as instances of the association of words with refer-
ents or images or 'action impulses'. Phase II came on strong, its
metaphor derived from communication theory rather than the
doctrine of association. But the problem of the lexicon, while
transformed, did not go away, even with the new metaphor of
communication and grammar. The doctrine of semantic markers
(Katz and Fodor [1963]), to be sure, brought the lexical problems
closer to the concern of the grammarians. But as Dale [1972] in
a comprehensive chapter on 'Semantic Development' observes,
'In the competition for least understood aspects of language acquisition, semantic development is surely the winner' (p. 131).

What was the communication metaphor? Miller, who had
such a major role in creating and explicating it, puts it well:

> The Communication metaphor focuses attention on the set of
> alternative signals . . . For human language, grammatical
> sentences are the signals to be analysed, and Chomsky in 1956
> accepted the Communication metaphor as the basis for his
> theory of generative grammar. A generative grammar is a
> set of rules that characterise all and only the admissible signals—
> the sentences—that can be communicated over a linguistic
> channel. The Communication metaphor called for a better
> theory of syntax, and generative grammar answered that call
> in an elegant and exciting way . . . The Communication
> metaphor had little interest in the growth of vocabulary.
> Words are merely the formal atoms that can be combined in
> grammatical sentences; it is the rules of combination, not the
> atomic elements, that capture the centre of the theoretical
> stage . . . Indeed it has little to say about meaning, and therein
> lies its weakness. Within the Communication metaphor, mean-
> ing is that ineffable something that should remain invariant
> under different encodings of the same message.

And Miller quite rightly concludes, 'The primacy of syntax may
be a valuable axiom for linguistics, but the primacy of semantics
is a better axiom for psychology.'

So forward to a third metaphor, and herein lies the route
for going more deeply into our problem. It may be called the
Computation model, or Phase III, and at its heart is the notion
that in learning words or meanings, either to utter or to comprehend them, one must master a set of component procedures
relating to their use—what is implied or presupposed, for example,
in using the word *bring*. At issue is *not* a set of procedures for

establishing under what conditions propositions using *bring* would be true, for example, as in *John brought the cheese*. Rather it is more like assembling a set of procedures for a computer program that would, when the sub-routines were put into action, be able to effect *bringing*. Meaning, then, becomes the capacity to compile 'the' set or some subset of the procedures relating to or presupposed in the action of *bringing*, such as 'hold', 'transport', 'keep in possession', etc.

Charles Sanders Peirce [1878] in his classic paper on the pragmatic theory of meaning—quite properly entitled 'How to Make our Ideas Clear'—proposed that the meaning of a word was the set of 'if-then' phrases into which it could be set. What is different about the Computation metaphor is that it specifies compilation only of procedures necessary for executing a meaning. The difference between compiling and executing is central. Davies and Isard [1972] propose a 'point of refusal' as the watershed between the two: Neither man nor machine can refuse to obey a command until the command has been understood. Thus compilation must occur automatically without conscious control by the listener; he cannot consciously refuse to understand a command (Miller, op. cit. p. 22), but he can plainly refuse to execute it or postpone its execution. It is at this crucial 'point of refusal' that compilation is completed and meaning established, whatever may happen later about execution and whether or not execution turns out to be appropriate to the expected outcome.

Plainly, natural languages do specify the 'procedures' to be compiled to establish meaning, and the acquisition of vocabulary involves understanding these, often first in action, as when we ask the young child, *Bring me the book*, and then *Bring me the shoe*. It is the test in action (or later paraphrase) that assures that meaning has been mastered. The process is not as well defined, of course, as in ordinary computing where one can state abstractly what any given procedure can do. A semantic theory of *computer* languages based on procedures characterises in general terms what programs are intended to do, and where possible decomposes the meanings of complex expressions into simpler expressions concerning performable operations. Since in the nature of things computer programs are necessarily well-formed propositions and natural-language propositions are mostly ill-formed, achieving an atomic level of simple performable operations may turn out to be harder and different and longer and only partially successful, and therefore the Oxford English Dictionary, for all its richness, does not succeed.

For all that, it seems to me to be worth exploring further the implications of this Phase III model for our understanding of how language and cognition interact. For if it is the case that language contains a set of implicit specifications for action and that this is its medium for specifying meanings, then there has indeed been added something of very great importance about how one initially learns and how one eventually uses language as an instrument. One initially *learns* language, if the account of procedural semantics is correct, by learning first how to *execute* the procedures that will later be necessary for establishing meaning. It is knowledge of these procedures that helps the language learner to 'discover' meaning in the lexicon and grammar of the language—because both are action-related. Indeed, I will insist that syntactical categories are no less action-relevant than the lexicon: how else can one interpret a case grammar containing categories like actor, object, action, location, modification, instrumentation, etc., to which the child is so sensitive (Greenfield, Smith and Laufer [in press]; Bloom [1970]). Plainly, the 'one-word-sentences', the holophrases, are appropriately combined with actions and action-gestures at the start of the young child's speaking career. It is this requirement of combination that makes appropriate prelinguistic experience necessary in early language acquisition. I have left out of the account for the moment the rôle of prior learning of *inter*actions, how one learns not only meanings related to *things*, but how one is inducted into the rules of exchange, as a prelinguistic prolegomenon to later mastery of the rules governing linguistic interaction.

There is a common origin that may account for the striking isomorphism of language and thought, the isomorphism that makes them instrumental to each other. Language, as De Laguna [1927] pointed out a long time ago, is in its origin and development a system for incorporating others in a plan of action, of enlisting conspecifics in the enterprise at hand. The selection pressure that led to present language was probably the requirement of better cooperation, which almost certainly meant the possibility of communicating in anticipation of, rather than merely as an accompaniment to, the action at hand. It meant, first, that language must relate as directly as possible to action and its structure. But it also meant, second, that the development of language was toward less context dependence, toward a form that involved greater explicitness and context independence so that messages could be decoded without knowledge of the situation in which they were uttered or of the intentions of the speaker. It was this that made possible the planning function, being able to talk about action in advance of its occurrence and out of the context in which the action would occur. The categories of action, then, had to be vicariously represented.

In a like vein, as Tolman [1932] was perhaps the most thorough in noting, thought too is an instrument for aiding action by anticipation, for laying out 'cognitive maps' of possible routes to goals, for scanning means-end possibility. Tolman saw its origin in 'vicarious trial and error' first in the presence of alternatives at a choice point and then, with correction, at choice points represented in thought. Thought, then, can be conceived as vicarious action using as its elements a set of combinable means-end relationships to be put together to guide 'real' action. Like language, it must provide representations of the procedures for carrying out actions. Where thought and language come together initially, then, is precisely in the regulation of action.

III

De Laguna makes much of one initial difference between animal cries and human language on the basis of their mode of separating *proclamation* and *command*. In the latter, they are separated, in the former, inextricably bonded.

> . . . the cry, so far as it proclaims at all, is able to announce only the general sort of situation—like 'danger' or 'prey'—while speech may *specify* and *analyse* the situation. The characteristic feature of human speech is that instead of being like the cry, a response to the total situation, having a direct affective value for the individual, it is a complex response, capable of discriminating the objective elements making up the situation . . . Instead of being limited like the alarm cry to the mere proclamation of 'danger', speech may announce.

She then goes on to point out that it could have taken a far different course—in the direction, for example, of an increasing differentiation of cries into types, a lexicon of appropriate danger warnings and other action signals. The form that it *did* take, separation, has had profound consequences.

For one, it probably makes possible the elaboration of meaning as embodied in the distinction between compilation and execution in the Phase III model discussed in the preceding section: the differentiation between understanding and doing. De Laguna proposes the hypothesis that the evolution of language (*and* I would argue of thought as well, the two taken as a joint system for the control of action) moved toward an elaboration of the proclamative feature, the differentiation of compilation from execution, of the cognitive map from the act derived from it. (I explore elsewhere [1972] the crucial rôle of freedom from predation and other pressures that may have made this separation possible and why increasingly elaborated play seems to be so crucial a feature of primate evolution, as well as of human language learning. It is, simply, because one must have some relief from immediate pressures in order to elaborate the proclamation feature of language in isolation from the requirements of action.)

De Laguna distinguishes four modes of proclamation that, while demonstrably *implicit* in animal cries, undergo further elaboration toward *explicitness* in the development of language: (1) presence or existence; (2) predication; (3) intention; and (4) accomplishments of intention. Predication differs from announcement of presence or existence in its selection of some feature of the event or act: the selected *comment* on a *topic*. Intention and accomplishment, of course, are ways of singling out direction and completion of action, and are selected predications on a cycle of action. The four modes of proclamation are a minimum set for guiding collaborative action: guides to what is present, what to select in what is present, what is to be done, and what is completed. What happens in human language is that these modes, as noted, become increasingly explicit and anticipatory to a degree beyond anything that can be seen elsewhere in nature.

Explicit proclamation depends upon freedom from 'the particular setting and context to determine the specific meaning for each occasion'. But how does the ability to represent situations in their absence or without action get accomplished? De Laguna proposes inhibition of action as a condition. 'Talking about it' and/or 'thinking about it' mean not doing it. But after all, inhibition or 'leisure' (see above) are background conditions and not the mechanisms that aided the emergence of thought as a system in which, to use De Laguna's words, 'language context comes more and more to take the place of perceptual context'. This progress is based upon at least two 'advances' in the mental apparatus of the hominids. The first, mentioned briefly earlier, is the ability to represent events, a matter as obscure today as when Aristotle broached it in the De Sensu. The second is probably a by-product of our mode of representation: 'Language singles out and specifies certain features relevant to the occasion of its use, but the features thus singled out remain in vital connection with what is not specified, but only presumed' (p. 109). It is this last feature, the entailment of a set of presuppositions, that provides the basis for a form of meaning that is context-independent, not interpretable by reference to an accompanying act or percept. We have already suggested that these presuppositions involved in meaning could be thought of as procedures in preparation for future action.

IV

We can now return to the central question. How does the use of language as a tool affect our mode of functioning? Is it so broad a question as to be absurd? Perhaps, if one interprets it too broadly.

Let me argue, first, that the *use* of language in ordinary discourse, without exploitation of its inherent structure of meaning and organisation, seems to have very little effect on the thought of its users beyond what might be called a 'species minimum'. Beyond that point, as indeed before it is reached, it is not the *possession* of language that matters, but rather the elaboration *of its use*. Given the concrete, intuitive use of language, limited to matters of fact, one seems (in attaining the 'species minimum') to go no further than Piaget's concrete operational phase in which one deals in concrete events in a logic that is *ad hoc*, local rather than universal, probabilistic, and not based on propositions related to each other by a principle of logical necessity. I shall comment shortly on the 'species minimum' which of course constitutes an enormous evolutionary step for *Homo*. For the moment, let me concentrate on the reaches of language use beyond it.

It is when one uses language beyond this 'minimum' level that it alters or, indeed, transforms the nature of the thought processes in a special way. The most general specification of such language use is its *movement toward context-free elaboration*. The most dramatic step in this direction was the development of notational systems that rendered spoken language into a graphic form—ideographs, syllabaries, alphabetic systems, and finally mathematical and computational languages.* But again, it is the effective use of

---

* Depiction by the use of art is doubtless of enormous importance, but beyond the scope of this paper.

these that works back to a transformation of thought, and indeed may do so by altering usage of the spoken language, by leading to the 'speaking of the written language' which is necessarily de-contextualised. In assessing the elaborated use of language as a tool of thought, it does not suffice to test for the *presence* in a speech sample of logical, syntactical, or even semantic distinctions, as Labov [1970] has done in order to determine whether non-standard Negro dialect is or is not impoverished. The issue, rather, is how language is being used, what in fact the subject is *doing* with his language.

I shall use data from several areas of research to illustrate what I mean by the elaborated use of language as an instrument of thought, and show how it may alter the nature of thought—at least pose some hypotheses about it.

Before turning to that matter, however, I had better make clearer what was intended by the 'species minimum' where language use is concerned. To begin with, it involves the kind of linguistic competence that is implied in such syntactically-centred Chomskian theories of language acquisition as McNeill's [1971] and would likewise include theories of language acquisition that had a semantic element in their base structures such as McCawley [1968], and notably Fillmore [1969] in his exposition of case grammar. Indeed, these theories operate on the assumption, more or less explicitly stated, that linguistic competence is innately based. Even Fillmore [1969, p. 21], working with a base structure of semantic universals, argues, 'The case notions comprise a set of universals, presumably innate, concepts which identify certain types of judgements human beings are capable of making about the events that are going on around them, judgements about such matters as who did it, who it happened to, and what got changed', categories like agent, instrument, recipient of action, result of action, location of action, etc. It is highly likely, if I may summarily express confidence in the research of Bloom [1970], Bowerman [1970], and Greenfield, Smith and Laufer [in press], that the categories in question, whether syntactic or semantic or operational, are characteristically used in prelinguistic commerce with objects and people—with the exception of trans-formational rules that permit, in Chomsky's [1965] classic sense, the transition from sound to sense. We do not begin to know (nor is it clear how to study) the contribution of such competence to man's cognitive life. Plainly, it has a great deal to do with pro-viding representations of events encountered, with giving a certain

shape to the category rules that are applied to the world in order
to reduce its complexity, and with the establishment of a common
base in terms of which people can learn to share experience. As
Luria [1961] so succinctly put it, 'By helping to define the required
cues, speech substantially modifies the child's perception and
permits the working-out of a system of stable differentiated
associations' (p. 29).

Beyond linguistic competence, there is yet another kind of
competence that Campbell and Wales [1970, p. 247] appropriately call 'communicative competence', the ability to make
utterances that are 'appropriate to the context in which they are
made', and presumably the ability to comprehend utterances in
the light of the context in which they are encountered. It involves
the kind of deictic relations involved in Piagetian decentration, as
well as a recognition not only of contexts but of the intentions
of speakers in a dialogue. As the philosopher Grice [1967] puts it,
there must be appreciation of a tripartite relationship in which
there is:

(i)   S's intention to produce a certain response, r, in A;
(ii) S's intention that A shall recognise S's intention (i) to do this;
(iii) S's intention that this recognition of S's intention (ii) is the
      reason, or part of it, for A's response, r.

A variety of psychologically oriented psycholinguists and socio-
linguists seems to agree that this area of study has been neglected
and that it is of central importance (e.g., Ryan [1973]; Marshall
[1970]; Hymes [1971]; Habermas [1970]; Cazden [1972]). For
our purposes, communicative competence involves the achievement of effective Piagetian 'concrete operations' (as noted), in
which language is serving as a mode for expressing and representing the structure of concrete thought about things and people.

The sphere in which language provides a new basis for the
human invention of new modes of thought is beyond either innate
linguistic competence or socially reinforced communicative competence. We shall label it *analytic competence*, and its principal
feature as with Piaget's formal operations (cf. Inhelder and Piaget
[1958]), is that it involves the prolonged operation of thought
processes exclusively on linguistic representations, on propositional
structures, accompanied by strategies of thought and problem-
solving appropriate not to direct experience with objects and
events but with ensembles of propositions. It is heavily metalinguistic in nature, in the sense of the use of this mode, involving

operations on the linguistic code, to assure its fit to sets of observations and it is strikingly the case that, more often than not, it generates new notational systems like mathematics, or more powerfully elaborated forms of the natural language like poetry. It is studied little.

Most work on language and cognition works with the universal 'species minimum' or with its pathologies (Goldstein [1943]; O'Connor and Hermelin [1963]). It is not only because of the educational implications of analytic competence, that we devote the remainder of the paper to it, but also because its study may reveal some general insights about the influence of language when it is used as an instrument of thought.

One deficiency in thought that is circumvented in analytic competence is that there is confusion between communication and its referent. As Vygotsky [1962, p. 129] notes:

> The word, to the child, is an integral part of the object it denotes. Such a conception seems to be characteristic of primitive linguistic consciousness. We all know the old story about the rustic who said he wasn't surprised that savants with all their instruments could figure out the size of the stars and their course—what baffled him was how they found out their names. Simple experiments show that preschool children 'explain' the names of objects by their attributes. According to them, an animal is called a 'cow' because it has horns, 'calf' because its horns are still small, 'dog' because it is small and has no horns; an object is called 'car' because it is not an animal. When asked whether one could interchange the names of objects, for instance, call a cow 'ink' and ink 'cow', children will answer no, 'because ink is used for writing and the cow gives milk'. An exchange of names would mean an exchange of characteristic features, so inseparable is the connection between them in the child's mind . . . We can see how difficult it is for children to separate the name of an object from its attributes, which cling to the name when it is transferred, like possessions following their owner.

The learning of language as communication is a qualitatively different activity from learning to use language internally as a technique of representation. But the language one has learned for use in communication has properties that can also be used as a program for dealing with things. The experiments of Martsignovskaya [1961] and Abramyan [1958] are particularly interesting in suggesting how language can help transcend the more rigid structures of perception, such as the dominance of figure over ground. Children will ordinarily respond to the figure on a ground —unless they are able to treat some property of the background in a way that renders it salient. They had a task of responding to airplane silhouettes, not their backgrounds. Now the task shifted, and they had to attend to the background. When, for example, they could say of grey and yellow backgrounds that they were 'cloudy days' and 'sunny days', they could stop responding to the airplane in the foreground by saying such things as, 'Airplanes fly on sunny days but not on cloudy ones.' The important thing about language as an instrument of thought is not that one can translate action or imagery into the new coin of words and sentences. Rather, it is that the new medium allows one to transform what one has put into it into a new and powerful form that is not possible by other means. The productive rules of language, its combinatorial richness, is potentially available as a means for going beyond experience. In this sense it is the powerful tool for innovation.

We certainly do not wish to imply that the 'rules' of language somehow become internalised and become the 'laws' of thought. The rules of a language are formal propositions 'invented' by linguists to generate its lawful utterances and to exclude those that are impermissible. But there are certain 'internalisations', and Vygotsky's discussion of these is worth revisiting. The principal means for developing correspondence between thought and language for Vygotsky is through 'inner speech', speech that becomes embodied in thought. The principal contribution of such inner speech is the gradual development of conceptualising rules in thought that correspond to grammatical categories. Outer speech develops first in the course of dialogue with adult figures. It presages the essentially social nature of speech in all its forms. With respect to inner speech (Vygotsky [1962, p. 13]):

[It] is speech for oneself; external speech is for others. It would indeed be surprising if such a basic difference in function did not affect the structure of the two kinds of speech. Absence of vocalisation per se is only a consequence of the specific nature of inner speech, which is neither an antecedent of external speech nor its reproduction in memory, but is, in a sense, the opposite of external speech. The latter is the turning of thought into words, its materialisation and objectification.

With inner speech the process is reversed: speech turns into inward thought. Consequently, their structures must differ.

Inner speech is a very rough first draft of outer speech. The principal difference between the two is that inner speech is dominated by 'predication' as a technique of abbreviation. 'As egocentric speech develops it shows a tendency toward an altogether specific form of abbreviation: namely, omitting the subject of a sentence and all words connected with it, while preserving the predicate' (p. 139). He concludes from this that inner speech goes on in a manner that resembles a dialogue between two people who have perfect understanding of what they are talking about to each other. They can, therefore, dispense with the subject and get directly to the predicate; like lovers or husbands and wives who share a common subject or people who have waited long for a bus and announce to one another, 'At last,' and need not say, 'The bus for which we have been waiting is coming at last.' Vygotsky writes, 'The key to this experimentally established fact is the invariable, inevitable presence in inner speech of the factors that facilitate pure predication: we know what we are thinking about, i.e., we always know the subject and the situation. . . . The predominance of predication is a product of development. In the beginning, egocentric speech is identical in structure with social speech, but in the process of its transformation into inner speech it gradually becomes less complete and coherent as it becomes governed by an almost entirely predicative syntax.'

Vygotsky's description is, in effect, a good account of how language and thought come to correspond at a poorly elaborated level of implicitness. At this level, there are no operations performed upon the linguistic representation itself, no metalinguistic activity by which one uses the structure and implications of the utterance to check or test the structure and connections in the event to which reference is being made. Recall that arguments about the Whorfian hypothesis usually took sides on two dichotomies. Was language a mould into which thought was poured, so to speak, or was it merely a cloak cut to fit the shape of thought? Secondly, did language have an obligatory effect on thought, or was it rather optional, 'predispositional' in the sense that if an 'idea' was highly codable it would simply be more likely to be used and/or understood? The brunt of the present argument is that, indeed, language can be either a mould or a cloak, depending upon how it is used, and by implication, we are dealing with an optional patterning

rather than an obligatory one. This interaction was succinctly put
a half-century ago by Sapir [1921] in his *Language*: '. . . the concept
once defined necessarily reacted on the life of its linguistic symbol,
encouraging further linguistic growth. We see this complex
process of the interaction of language and thought actually
taking place under our eyes. The instrument makes possible the
product, the product refines the instrument. . . . Not until we
own the symbol do we feel that we hold a key to the immediate
knowledge or understanding of the concept' (p. 17). For once the
symbol is available, it then becomes possible to explore its pre-
suppositional structure, to compile the procedures related to it,
to examine the fit between the extended meaning derived
linguistically with the experiential tests that can be performed
directly on the referent. My only quarrel with Sapir is that this
does *not* occur either necessarily or automatically at all levels of
language use, a point to be developed later.

What is distinctive in 'analytically competent' language use
is that its process of compiling presuppositions requires more
ordered operations on a set of formal categories. A description of
the difference between such activity and the usual functional
processing of events is provided by Bruner, Goodnow, and Austin
[1956, p. 5–6]:

> Formal categories are constructed by the act of specifying the
> intrinsic attribute properties required by the members of a
> class. Such categories have the characteristic that one can
> state reliably the diacritica of a class of objects or events short
> of describing their use. The formal properties of science are a
> case in point. Oftentimes the careful specification of defining
> properties even requires the construction of special 'artificial'
> languages to indicate that common-sense functional categories
> are not being used. The concept 'force' in physics and the word
> standing for the functional class of events called 'force' in
> common-sense do not have the same kind of definition . . . The
> development of formalisation is gradual. From 'things I can drive
> this tent stake with' we move to the concept 'hammer' and from
> there to 'mechanical force', each step being freer of definition
> by specific use than the former . . . The development of formal
> categories is tantamount to science making . . . Indeed, it is
> characteristic of highly elaborated cultures that symbolic
> representations of formal categories and formal category systems
> are eventually developed without reference to the classes of

environmental events that the formal categories 'stand for'. Geometry provides a case in point, and while it is true that its original development was contingent upon the utilitarian triangulation systems used for redividing plots after floods in the Nile Valley, it is now the case that geometers proceed without regard for the fit of their formal categories to specific empirical problems.

Both Vygotsky [1962] and Inhelder and Piaget [1958] have interesting perspectives on the operations used in dealing with 'formal categories'. The latter authors note (p. 251),

Finally, in formal thought there is a reversal in the direction of thinking between *reality* and *possibility* in the subjects' method of approach. *Possibility* no longer appears merely as an extension of an empirical situation or of actions actually performed. Instead it is *reality* that is now secondary to *possibility*. Henceforth, they conceive of the given facts as that sector of a set of possible transformations that has actually come about; for they are neither explained nor even regarded as facts until the subject undertakes verifying procedures that pertain to the entire set of hypotheses compatible with a given situation. In other words, formal thinking is essentially hypothetico-deductive. By this we mean that the deduction no longer refers to perceived realities but to hypothetical statements, i.e., it refers to propositions which are formulations of hypotheses which postulate facts or events independently of whether or not they actually occur . . . The most distinctive property of formal thought is this reversal of direction between *reality* and *possibility*; instead of deriving a rudimentary theory from the empirical data as is done in concrete inferences, formal thought begins with a theoretical synthesis implying that certain relations are necessary and thus proceeds in the opposite direction.

For Vygotsky [1962] the crucial difference in formal thought (he used the expression 'scientific concepts') is the interconnectivity of the concepts in formal thought in contrast to their looser connection in spontaneous thought—likening the former to positions on a sphere marked with a set of totally connected coordinates of latitude and longitude. In effect, the point is the same as with Inhelder and Piaget [1958], and with Bruner, Goodnow, and Austin [1956]: the achievement of a fully developed set of possible alternatives with selection rules for combining them to achieve given predictions that can then be tested against reality.

One can obviously cite ample evidence from studies of aphasia, of subnormality, of language development to show the difficulty of acquiring and the vulnerability to injury of such formal or hypo-thetico-deductive thinking. Unfortunately, there are as yet no close studies of the acquisition or decay of high level thinking, save the studies of adolescence by Inhelder and Piaget [1958] whose conclusions on the importance of 'possibility' we have just cited. Their argument is that he who thinks in formal terms employs operations that can be described in terms of the sixteen binary operations of propositional calculus. It is highly unlikely, of course, that the processes underlying such thinking are anything like the operations of affirmation, negation, conjunction, in-compatibility, disjunction, etc. But they plainly are different from those that come naturally to a language user whose competence is limited to ordinary day-to-day exchange. Inhelder and Piaget [1958] speculate that the beginnings of propositional thinking may be stimulated by the requirement, as we approach adulthood, of having to take on rôles and, in doing so, being forced to think of the connected set of rôles to which ours relate. Doubtless, as many anthropologists have affirmed, this is an important goad to elaborated thought. When the Bernsteinian [1970] 'expanded' or universal code fails to take root in sub-cultures where poverty produces a sense of helplessness, the mechanism may be the cutting down of the sense of possibility that nurtures more formal operations (cf. Bruner [1970]).

There is something curiously unnatural about the kinds of operations to which we are referring; they are candidates for what Simon [1970] has called the 'sciences of the artificial'. In closing this already too lengthy speculative essay, let me finally suggest what I think produces this 'unnatural' elaboration of intellectual activity, why it does not come automatically through language use. I take my lead from a recent paper by McNeill [1971] entitled 'The Two-fold Way for Speech'. He begins with the classical distinction made by Lashley [1951], '. . . syntax is not inherent in the words employed or in the ideas expressed. It is a generalised [cerebral] pattern imposed on the specific acts as they occur' (p. 119), and 'This is the essential problem of serial order: the existence of generalised schemata of action which determine the specific sequence of specific acts, acts which in themselves or in their associations seem to have no temporal valence' (p. 122). The object of McNeill's paper is to explore the relation between the speech rate, the rate at which underlying elementary sentences that can contain a semantic load are formed, and the rate at which cognitive processes go forward. By a variety of experimental and mathematical methods, he comes to the conclusion that the sentence-generating time (between 1 and 2 seconds) is about the same as the time it takes to shift attention from one feature of the environment to another (Broadbent [1954], Treisman [1960]). He concludes: 'Thus, one can speculate, the brain processes for constructing underlying sentences operate in such a manner as to produce new foci of attention at this rate. In this sense speech can be said to be the bridge between conscious awareness and largely unconscious cognitive operations, such as identification, classification, and storage' (p. 24). The argument, you will see, is based on the relationship between the semantic encoding required in sentence formation and the attention required to extract the information from perceptual input or from storage in memory, though he does not distinguish between the two.

The point that I wish to make is that it is this close coupling between ordinary speech and everyday cognition that creates the 'artificiality' of using language as an instrument of thought beyond this level. And here we can go back to the model that Miller [1973] is proposing, that meaning requires the preliminary compiling of procedures which can then be run off (if needed) in a correct serial order. Like Lashley [1951] and like McNeill's derivation from Lashley just cited, Miller postulates that the compiling in advance of speaking or acting need not reflect serial order. Language used in the ordinary way is accompanied by thought processes that simultaneously activate a pool of words that are then put in an appropriate order for speech—and do so steadily and reliably although Spoonerisms and kindred speech errors suggest that the process is not always successful. Now, for a speaker finally to gain analytic competence with the language used as a tool, he must do far more than retrieve a *pool* of words in response to what he finds at his focus of attention, a pool that can then be put in proper sequence by 'grammatical processes'. Thought now serves not only to provide a quick compilation, but demands a serial order and a choice among alternatives not present to attention. As McNeill (p. 3) puts it, 'Thought has no intrinsic order, Lashley believed, and therefore cannot be used to explain the organisation of speech'. I would argue that formal thought, geared to the manipulation of explicit, context-free propositions, comes increasingly to mirror the serial requirement of the linguistic system. One thinks in propositions to operate appropriately upon them. Orderly, 'logical' thinking, moreover, uses the *possible* in just the sense that Inhelder and Piaget intend. In this sense, thinking formally involves consideration of the full range of possible grammatical cases that might characterise a thought sequence. And here again, Fillmore's case grammar provides an excellent example. Thus, when a speaker of developed analytic competence begins a sequence of thought, he will take into account the range and order of such relevant matters as agent, action, direct object of action, instrumentality, possession, and so forth. And if the notational system is an artificial language, say a form of mathematics, the speaker will similarly employ the permissible operations of the mathematical system as the mode of thought, and do so with an appropriate serial ordering. The linguistic *system* and not the external reality is what determines the mental operations and their order. Nor need it be very highbrow, though it becomes so with practice. My favourite example of the two approaches, both at a fairly low level, is the difference in response to the request to name the States of the Union—the difference between those who start, 'Maine, New Hampshire, Vermont, Massachusetts, Rhode Island, Connecticut . . .' and those who go, 'Alabama, Alaska, California, Connecticut . . .' It goes without saying that the processing rate proposed by McNeill for sentences is *much* too rapid for the kind of thought processes that must accompany linguistically determined analytic thought, for it is no longer preceded by rapid attentional shifts. Rather, and here lies its artificiality, it may well be that it takes a day of work to get two pages through the typewriter.

How would one test for the shift? What is its bearing on research? Three suggestions. The first has to do with word association and word use, and the process on the older side of the syntagmatic-paradigmatic shift. My guess is that this shift is followed later, and only in some people, by a shift from paradigmatic to analytic—the use of formal structures to generate associates. In a like vein, it will be found to manifest itself in hypothesis generation in tasks like those used by Duncker [1945], by Bruner, Olver, and Greenfield [1966], and by Maier [1930]. Secondly, I would suggest that studies similar to those of Inhelder and Piaget [1958] be carried out to assess the manner in which the structured and 'possible' categories of language affect thought—even using a cross-cultural perspective of the kind found in Greenfield [1968] and in Cole, Gay, Glick, Sharp *et al.* [1971]. And finally, I would make a plea for that neglected third branch of developmental linguistics: pragmatics, which I would define as the study of what language using does to its users.

I promised a remark about the elaboration in thought of poetic activity. Roman Jakobson is currently at work on a volume that will one day have the title 'The Poetry of Language and the Language of Poetry' in which he makes the point that poetry involves, in its formal aspect, as demanding a set of rules for structuring poetic discourse, as mathematical systems and, because of the requirements of regulating phonological and prosodic features, perhaps more complex sets of rules. The professional poet comes to think in terms of these in his processing of experience. They provide not only the rules but also the realm of the possible into which his skill takes him.

SPEAKER'S INTRODUCTION

It is indeed a strange thing to talk on the subject of language and thought. One would have thought that everything sensible that could be said has been said. I have tried in my paper to get away from the well-tried notion of the effect of language on thought, which was often referred to as the coming together of two streams, by looking at a different kind of metaphor. This comes out of my interest in the evolution of language and concerns the use of language as an instrument of thought. Assuming that thought is a way of stumbling along towards a given objective, what you do in order to reach that objective is to vary the means, the linguistic process. You say it to yourself, you re-formulate it. We can treat language in the same way as in a parallel study of mine into the effect of the use of tools on human skill and human thought.

Now after the changes in fashion in linguistics and psychological approaches to language which I mention in my paper it seems to me we have come to the point where it is being realised that what really needs to be explored—in linguistics proper and in its relations to psychology—is semantics. As it happens I think myself that the route into language and learning or language and imbeddedness into society is pragmatics. This leads me on to propose that there is in the child not only a linguistic competence, not only a communicative competence (and I am ignoring the problems associated with both notions), but also a third something. This is something very special and consists not only of learning language and learning how to use language appropriately, but then of learning how to use the language as a representation of reality and how to go on for long periods of time manipulating the language in thought before having to read back to the situation. I emntion the work of Inhelder and Piaget which interests me very much in this context. This third stage I call analytic competence.

Discussant: *Colin Fraser*

Let me say how pleased I was to be invited to comment on the paper by Professor Bruner since I assumed it was bound to be a very rich mixture, as has been the case. My pleasure was somewhat reduced, however, when I discovered more recently that the paper was a discussion of relationships between language and thought. I immediately felt that I should have been ruled out as a discussant on the grounds that I have a chronic inability to understand general discussions on the relationship between language and thinking.

I used to feel that the problem with discussions of language and thinking was that of making explicit what was meant by 'thinking'. 'Language' seemed to be much clearer. By means of notions like features, phonemes, morphemes, etc., one could make explicit what one meant by language, but no one seemed to be in a position (and I think this is a reasonable claim) to make explicit what was implied by thought. Thinking had to be defined in a largely intuitive 'we all know what we mean' way.

More recently, though, I have felt that particularly in the context of an analysis of the relationship between language and thinking there is also a problem in deciding what is meant by 'language'. There seems to be a very relevant ambiguity in the use of the term 'language' here. On the one hand, there is language in a broad sense, in which we take for granted the fact that language includes thinking. (After all, many people have considered it worthwhile asking 'Is thought possible without language?', presumably because that seems a plausible possibility, but few have asked 'Is language possible without thought?', presumably beacuse they have taken it for granted it is not). On the other hand, in the context of discussing the relationship between language and thinking we seem to be using language in a narrower sense. We are implying that we can talk about something that is opposed to or different from thought, and it would be very helpful if we could begin by defining the two terms, language and thought, independently, and perhaps use a third term such as 'language in action' or 'language in use', or even 'speech', to characterise the combination of the two.

So, for example, to over-simplify grossly and to horrify the linguists, if language in a broad sense is conventionally analysed as phonology plus syntax plus semantics, it would be very convenient if we could say that, in the narrow sense, we shall treat language as phonology and syntax and hand semantics over to thought or cognition. Since I realise that that is fraught with very many difficulties, let me try an alternative. If language in the broad sense is surface structure plus deep structure, it would be very convenient if we could say that, in the narrow sense, language will be surface structure and deep structure will be thought. Again, this is a gross over-simplification; it says nothing, for example, about what the equipment is—and whether it is linguistic or cognitive or a mixture of the two—that takes you from deep structure to surface structure and back again. Nonetheless, it strikes me that this approach to separating the two may not be totally far-fetched. If one looks, for example, at developmental psycholinguistics one encounters an increasingly 'Piagetian' view of the early development of language, whereby writers such as Macnamara [1972] and Slobin [1972] seem to be saying that there are non-linguistic cognitive categories and cognitive achievements that precede and are necessary for linguistic development and that these non-linguistic categories are very much the early deep structure. Similarly, if in linguistics one takes case grammar and asks about the nature of the categories in deep structure (actor, agent, and the like): are they linguistic in any narrow sense or are they cognitive in a much broader sense? So one might find some value in this over-simplified distinction. At the very least, in this day and age, the rallying cry 'Language really is surface structure!' has an appealing heretical ring to it.

I have started with these general remarks because in going through the paper I feel that I am in sympathy with Professor Bruner's arguments when I can persuade myself that he is separating language from thought in a non-overlapping way. One instance is in my interpretation of the argument that the really distinctive contribution of language to thought lies with the contribution to formal thinking and formal operations of what is called 'analytic competence'. On the other hand, the points at which I either feel that I am not willing to go along with the paper or where I feel uncertain about the argument are often those where I feel that the discussion of language is including those cognitive operations that should be contrasted with language. This conference is attempting to relate the study of language to educational questions. But before discussing the educational implications of Professor Bruner's complex paper I would like to feel we had got the basic concepts straight. So let me move through the paper and indicate some of the themes that I think require further discussion.

In the first section of the paper, I agree with Professor Bruner's point about the one-directional emphasis in discussions of language and thought and I hope my comments about the ambiguity of 'language' throw some light on why this has been the case.

In the second section of the paper, let me object, almost for ideological reasons, to one of the metaphors which Professor Bruner has borrowed from George Miller. It strikes me that to describe Phase II, whether one sees it as inspired by information theory or as inspired by syntactic transformational grammar, in terms of a communication metaphor is to extend the notion of the metaphor quite unreasonably. I feel either view had very little to say about communication. If one wants to label the metaphor, one might describe it as a combination or seriation metaphor as opposed to an association one. A communication metaphor, I think, only applies to some of the most recent, let us say, sociolinguistic studies of language.

Bruner I think it had to do basically with the title of that earlier book called *Language and Communication*.

Fraser That is right. As I say, I feel that it has very little to do with communication.

Bruner I agree.

Fraser In this second section of the paper, the argument that Professor Bruner is putting forward is that meaning is established in terms of a computation metaphor and particularly in terms of compilation rather than execution, if I understood him correctly. That is, meaning is established by compiling a set of procedures. Here, can I ask a couple of questions in order to try to push the analogy a little bit further, to find out how far the analogy should be pushed? From my limited knowledge of computers, I gather that compilation, or a compiler, is used when instructions in a higher order language are being broken down into much more detailed, much more specific instructions in a lower level machine language. It is a fine analogy for distinguishing compilation from the actual execution of the program, but can I ask if the analogy does make use of the notion of both higher order language and the lower level machine language and, if so, what is it in the analysis of meaning that corresponds to the higher order language? That is, meaning is apparently produced when the compiler has got to work, but what is it that one starts with? Secondly, although, in theory, a compiler should in Professor Bruner's terms produce the meaning in the program, I gather that in practice, compilers being what they are, computer users very often only feel or only know that the compiler has got it right—that is that the compiler really has got the meaning— when they have tried out the program. Apparently compilers can go wrong in lots of ways, and it is very difficult to be sure that what you hoped would be there really is there, and the best way of checking this is to carry out some sort of dry-run. I wonder is that part of the analogy? Do we have to add an 'ideal compiler' to the more familiar 'ideal speaker-hearer'?

In the third section of the paper, Professor Bruner argues that a crucial feature in the evolution of language is the elaboration of proclamation, which relates to the previous point in that proclamation, separates or helps separate compilation from execution. And proclamation implies freedom of the utterance from the specific context. Here, it strikes me that language is being used in the broad sense. That is, language and thought are being used as a joint system for the control of action and therefore I am not sure whether the enriching of proclamation is due to the evolution of language in a narrow sense or the evolution of non-linguistic cognitive elements.

In the fourth part of his paper, Bruner asks his basic question, 'How does the use of language affect our mode of functioning?' He argues that its most distinctive effect is that it makes possible the attainment of an analytic competence which permits us to think in a particularly abstract, hypothetical fashion. Analytic competence, in my interpretation, involves the fusing of language in the narrow sense, presumably syntax in particular, with thought.

Analytic competence is sharply distinguished from functioning which involves the language 'species minimum'. I must admit to some surprise at the lumping together under this label of the Chomsky–McNeill concept of linguistic competence and the Hymes–Campbell and Wales concept of communicative competence. Of course, if one thinks that linguistic competence is, in some strong sense, innately determined then it is easy to think of it as part of a species minimum. Alternatively, one might feel that some notions of linguistic competence, for example, the ability to judge the grammaticality of sentences completely removed from context, are such restricted notions as to be hardly worth quibbling about. But the much broader notion of communicative competence is a different matter. I would have thought that it is sufficiently complex in nature, sufficiently slow in its development and, in many people, eventually developed in only partial form, that to describe it as part of a 'minimum' seems strange.

But, however one wishes to label them, the argument is that linguistic and communicative competences in themselves do not ensure the attainment of functioning comparable to Piagetian formal operations. These require the structures of a language system to be used as the actual tools for thought. To me, this argument, coming as it does from Bruner, seems to imply a surprisingly Piagetian view of the relation between thought and language, and the claim that it is in analytic competence that language is most important as an *intrapersonal* tool for thought seems quite acceptable.

An interesting point about analytically competent language use is its 'unnaturalness'. Using a suggestion of McNeill's, in a paper which I must admit I have not seen, Bruner proposes that naturalness in language use involves a close relationship between sentence generating time and switching time in attention. But, far from occurring at one- or two-second intervals, formal, hypothetical statements—particularly worthwhile ones—can take a long time to produce. The idea of relating sentence generation to attentional processes seems worth pursuing. I trust, however, that the present proposal is not totally dependent on something between one and two seconds being accepted as *the* solution to the measurement of switching time in attention. I would have thought that recent discussions, such as Moray [1969] would suggest that for present purposes it would be better to fudge the issue of what the minimal switching time is, if indeed there is such a thing. One might add that a more general study of attentional factors as they influence speech comprehension and production would seem to have obvious educational relevance.

This then is one topic that we might well take up in further discussion. The other questions that I think deserve attention are: some of the unexplored problems in language–cognition relationships Bruner points to in the early part of his paper; the analysis of meaning in terms of computation, particularly compilation; the analysis of proclamation and its relation to context independence; the concepts of species minimum and analytic competence; and the question that I started with, namely, in the context of a discussion of language and thought, what *is* the most useful way of defining language?

Having rôle-played a psychologist discussing language and thinking, let me allow myself one final comment as the social psychologist that I really am. I wonder if language as an intrapersonal tool for thought is anywhere near as important as language as an innerpersonal tool. Surely the real impact of language on thought comes via the language of other people. So that while I sympathise with Halliday's desire to avoid spending his time peering into the head of a single person, I think that the most fruitful approach to the study of language will involve us in attempts to peer into the heads of at least two people simultaneously.

[The film 'Early Words' was then shown to the Seminar by J. S. Bruner.]

GENERAL DISCUSSION

Sloman The audible parts of language belong to a very complex mechanism involving intentions, actions, thoughts, successes and failures, etc. It was obvious from the film that what was going on every time the child produced a word was just the tiny tip of the iceberg. The child has to cope with some pretty complex geometrical problem-solving to do things like seeing three-dimensional objects and recognising its mother from all sorts of other faces, from all sorts of angles. You cannot realise how difficult this is until you try to get a robot to do it. That is why artificial intelligence is so important for psychology. The child is relating some kind of intention—heaven knows how it is to be represented— to eat, go outside, call its mother, play some complex game—to a set of resources it has, its arms and legs and the ability to move them around, linguistic abilities. Also in some cases, the ability to understand much more complex sentences than it has the ability to produce, as we saw once or twice in the film.

Marie Clay   I recall something from I. A. Richards' review of Jean Charles' book in the *Harvard Educational Review* in which he said that the first time the child comes to examine meaning in any detailed way is when he is faced with the early reading situation.

Griffiths   It seems to me a priori that people make a great deal of use of imagery in solving complex problems and that perhaps the way in which language is used in solving complex problems in analytical thought is by providing one with some kind of way in which one can make up for short-term memory problems. One can write down sentences which tell one some particular aspect of the problem that one has to come back to later on.

Margaret Donaldson   It is a very sophisticated thing to do to think about the meaning of utterances, to want to conceive of an utterance as having a meaning. There is a distinction between asking 'What do you mean?', which some children can do quite readily, and 'What does that statement mean?', i.e. considering what the meaning of the language is.

Bruner   The amusing thing about Carol Chomsky's monograph (1969 was that it indicated that children do not have this automatic 'I've got to the age of 4, I know the grammar'. But more substantively it showed that children can understand relations and operations without controlling the particular language forms to describe them.

Margaret Donaldson   I think that is true of a great many simple syntactic forms among pre-school children. You do not have to look at more difficult and complex aspects of language among older children.

Joan Tough   I do not think we are paying enough attention to the influence of outside factors. For example, the meaning of the thought *mother* is not carried by the language, but the language within the child is in fact defining certain pathways and certain patterns and associations. Within the developing period from about 2 onwards what the language does for the child is to induce certain attentions, expectancies, searches both in the outside here and now, and in what is within him from the past. And any language can do this.

Nathan   I have a methodological question. I take it that in your analytic competence you are describing a shift of some kind. Now is there not something improper in using as diagnostic capital the same categories both in talking about analytic competence and in studying it?

Bruner I think it is acceptable. What one looks for, after all, in making a judgement is forms of error. There are lots of ways of solving a problem: you do not find out about what is wrong until the child makes an error, and the error tells you the diagnostic side.

Margaret Donaldson Piaget does not distinguish two things that should be distinguished: the ability to conceive of something as possible and the ability to work out systematically what the possibilities are. The first of these exists in some sense very much in fantasy. But children go beyond this in developing the second ability.

Bernstein I am not too happy with the notion of analytic competence and relating it to the child's imagination. What seems to me important is the *context*: what counts as the context. In the film it struck me that the whole of the interaction between mother and child went on against a complex set of presuppositions which created some kind of frame they have learned to share. It is the creation of this frame that is important. It seems to me that we are once again seeing two sets of theories confronting one another. The one set tries to dig up universals—developmental, genetic theories—experimental as opposed to clinical, and particularly a definition of what counts as the context. The other set take the first for granted—they are concerned with examining the principles underlying variations and have quite different definitions of what the context is. I think that in this afternoon's discussion the universalists have had the floor and they have defined the context. What we need to do is to try to bring these two approaches together.

Other points were made in the discussion by:
  I. Morris
  C. Fraser
  Ruth Clark

ADDENDUM

After the Seminar J. S. Bruner with the help of Karen L. Peterson revised this paper 'Language as an Instrument of Thought'. Unfortunately it was not found possible to replace Bruner's first paper by the Bruner–Peterson revision (as Bruner himself wished) but in order to indicate to the reader that there has been some change in Bruner's own thinking in this area since the Seminar an abstract of the revised paper is presented at the end of this volume. This abstract has been written by the editor.

4

Language and Reading: Research Trends

MARGARET M. CLARK

The focus of psychological research into reading has until recently been mainly on the negative aspects of levels of illiteracy, causes of failure in reading and remedial techniques. This is unfortunate not only because of the wide range of aspects of reading left unstudied, but also because of the possibility of erroneous conclusions based on a too exclusive concentration on the failures and those with difficulties.

This emphasis may lead both to a mistaken evaluation of the significance of certain disabilities found in those who learn to read only with difficulty, and to a limited conception of the skill which is to be defined as reading. Studies such as *The Trend of Reading Standards* by Start and Wells,[1] exemplifying among other things this focus on comparative levels of literacy at different ages and times, will contribute little to the understanding of reading though they may alert public attention to the need for research. Not only is this type of investigation too general for the crucial factors, even in the school situation, to be identified with sufficient precision, but also the type of measuring instrument devised for the survey approach is too crude to focus satisfactorily on the various facets of reading ability in the adult fluent reader. Such studies of large selected groups will, therefore, even if carefully planned and executed, make only a very limited contribution to improvement in the teaching of reading.

Readiness and Reading

Again, analysis of reading readiness as studied so far seems to have contributed little to the more effective teaching of reading. Disappointingly little of value has been discovered from this area of study.[2] It is salutary to bear in mind the study by Krippner who describes a young child, already a fluent reader at an early age, who would have been declared unready to begin reading tuition had he been subjected to the type of reading readiness test then in vogue. There is probably no single aspect of the reading readiness test battery which is an absolute barrier to learning to read for all children under all conditions of tuition. Many readiness tests have used perceptual tasks not involving the specific characteristics of print but of visual and auditory symbols; transferability has then been assumed. The existence of such tests has led teachers to assume an 'unreadiness' in many children and coupled with this a need for perceptual training programmes to prepare the child for initial reading instruction. Attention has been distracted away from, rather than directed towards, the specific characteristics of written communication and the need for appropriately directed instruction.

Similarly, evidence of failure on tests of auditory discrimination in backward readers has led to the highlighting of ability in phonemic discrimination as a significant factor in reading progress.[3] Studies of phonemic discrimination have, however, tended to be based on judgement of similarity or difference in pairs of simple words or nonsense syllables. Recently attention has turned to the additional factors in the test of auditory discrimination. For the test the child must listen, hold the sequence of sounds in memory, make a comparison of them and on this basis make a decision of similarity or difference. Failure in the test could be influenced by any of these aspects: where words are used, familiarity with the words might be an additional factor. In an ongoing study in London, Ontario, where the test involves judgement on pairs of phonemes, a high overall performance was found even in young school beginners and an analysis of errors indicated that *few* phoneme pairs were contributing to the test difficulty. Hardy[4] concludes in her report that in some of the popular tests of auditory discrimination, factors other than auditory discrimination are being measured and that exaggerated estimates are being made of auditory discrimination difficulties. The young fluent readers in this writer's present study had no difficulty with the *task* of auditory discrimination nor indeed with the *test* the purpose of which they quickly grasped. Their skill may, however, be in the linguistic area rather than in the more refined sphere of auditory discrimination. Though attention is now being directed to print and its characteristics in the visual area, and speech and its characteristics in the auditory area, it is important not to over-simplify the analysis. A child's difficulties and lack of readiness for reading may be a result of failure to discriminate like-sounding speech patterns or may be the result of a failure to differentiate like-sounding words. The difficulty may, however, be aggravated by, if not caused by, an emphasis in the instructional strategies on inappropriate techniques without direct transfer to the task, which result in the child's progress being arrested.

An analysis of fluent readers and of the association between certain characteristics of readiness and success by particular learning strategies is important. Studies in this area require to be extended to the characteristics of auditory discrimination which are exemplified in children who learn to read easily and fluently. These must, however, be considered within the context of the children's language performance and awareness.

Reading readiness tests do tap language, but where they do, as stated by Wilkinson,[5] they tend to check vocabulary rather than syntax. Wilkinson feels that a systematic study of the relationship between reading and pre-reading oracy is an important aspect of study and that the ability to read is largely dependent on the skill in spoken language which the learner already possesses. Using a language involves knowing a great deal about what is likely to follow at any point in a spoken message, that is a knowledge of sequential probabilities on all levels of language.[6] Though many would feel that a child's prior grasp of sequential probabilities in oral language will be a significant factor in 'readiness' for reading there is scope for systematic longitudinal studies of children in an attempt to relate their pre-school appreciation of language to their development of an understanding of the reading task. Clearly such studies would require to take into account the effects of different approaches to the initial teaching of reading.

As greater understanding of the *oral* language development of children has resulted from an analysis of their errors and self-corrections in speech, so also in reading it is important that in the early oral *reading behaviour* of children, their errors and self-corrections be monitored. In reading, taped records of the error patterns and self-corrections of different children under different initial approaches to learning to read would seem to be a fruitful line of enquiry in the hope of developing both a more sensitive teaching of reading and an analysis of the significant factors in language readiness for reading.[7] The work of Clay on the development of concepts of print in young children, and her research (in progress) on the reconstruction of sentences made by young school beginners when faced with tasks beyond their short-term memory are relevant to this aspect. It may be, as some researchers have suggested, that the factors that correlate highly with early reading success are different from those that correlate with later success. More attention, however, needs to be focused on whether, or to what extent, there is a significantly different relationship at different stages in the learning task or whether this discrepancy is most marked when the initial reading materials give fewest linguistic cues for decoding.

The oral language of young children is, however, not the only relevant aspect for study when analysing readiness for reading. Consideration must also be given to the other aspects of language awareness which are significantly related to success in the reading task, whether these can be systematically taught, and which approaches in the teaching are most successful. It is important to bear in mind that anticipation of the likely completion of a sentence or word is not dependent only on comprehension but operates also below that level in the area referred to as the intermediate reading skills.[8] This is another fruitful line of further investigation at different developmental levels and under different conditions. 'Reading' for Smith[9] involves *predicting* one's way through a passage of text eliminating some alternatives in advance on the basis of knowledge of the redundancy of language and acquiring just enough visual information to eliminate the alternatives remaining. As in oral language, so also in reading, anticipation plays an important part. Indeed Goodman has referred to reading as a 'Psycholinguistic guessing game'.[10]

If one approaches the teaching of reading from an analysis of the skills and knowledge the child has already acquired when he begins learning to read, and of the additional knowledge and skills required for fluent reading, one may be led to the conclusion that the present approaches to the initial teaching of reading miss some of the crucial features required for the development of such a skill. Indeed they may focus mistakenly on the very features which characterise unsuccessful rather than successful reading. Too much emphasis may be placed on training skills such as precise visual scanning of letters or words, while the important features may indeed be *discrimination* and *anticipation* rather than identification.

Significant also within the area of language readiness and the initial teaching of reading is an analysis of the extent to which a child's success in learning to read may be influenced not only by his competence in the language of the reading materials but also the language of reading instruction employed by the teacher. The studies of Reid[11] and Downing[12] have shown the limited grasp of the language of reading instruction by young school beginners.

In learning to read, young children are confronted with a complicated array of auditory and visual language concepts which are an integral part of the instructional language used by primary teachers. Little is known of the normal development of these concepts, the order in which they should be introduced, and which of them should be mastered before critical reading skills are presented. (M. I. Hardy)[13]

A distinction must be made between the language awareness required in order to learn to appreciate the significant characteristics of print, and the language sophistication required in order to make progress when subjected to the complicated, and often imprecise, terminology in some early reading instruction. The solution may be neither to delay reading instruction nor to teach the language of reading instruction but to by-pass these language deficiencies by a more direct approach. Precise 'examples' and 'contrasts', as these apply in print—evidence, rather than instruction may be supplied and the child be encouraged to differentiate without use of the words 'same' and 'different' (Smith 1971). Studies of the language of instruction used by teachers and the extent to which it is related to the level of sophistication of the language awareness of the children taught by them would be a valuable extension of the work of Reid and Downing.

In turning attention to the importance of language in learning to read, the reading task must be defined with sufficient precision for instructional strategies to be devised. Children usually learn to read in school and therefore in a group situation; certain features being common to all such situations, there is thus a possibility that certain crucial variables may be overlooked and others erroneously thought to be crucial. For this reason the present writer felt that a study of young fluent readers might shed some light on an aspect of the development of skilled reading which might otherwise not have been appreciated; the characteristics of the children themselves and of their learning environment —in this case the home.

A combination of the types of studies suggested above could lead to an analysis of the learning task, the learning situation, and the extent to which these interrelate to determine the progress of a child in his initial experiences in the reading situation. The readiness of the child is only one aspect; the preparedness of the school to suit the instruction to the needs of both task *and* child are worthy of more detailed investigation. Clearly language readiness and reading is one area where coordinated studies using the skills and techniques of both educational psychologists and linguists should lead to more penetrating and significant investigations.

Language Studies and Approaches to Teaching Reading

Word counts of the most frequently used words in adult reading were followed by word counts of children's speech or writing as a means of providing simplified content for children's early reading materials. Many reading schemes popularly in use present frequent repetition of such words in 'simple' sentence structures with progressive introduction of new words assumed to be already in the child's speaking vocabulary. Such an approach should assist the child's progress by presenting discrimination of words already known in spoken form; by enabling the word forms used to be of widely different visual patterns and by increasing motivation as a result of the utilisation of more meaningful material. Restriction of the initial reading experiences of a child to phonically regular words or word-like patterns enables a more systematic instruction in the structure and pattern of words to be developed and provides the child earlier with an independent, if limited, code-breaking strategy. Problems arise, however, in providing children with meaningful and certainly with significantly meaningful reading material when only 'regular' words are used. Many teachers use a combination of phonic and look-and-say approaches, differing in their emphasis and in the extent to which they base their phonic instruction on a systematic phonic programme or on incidental guidance as required. Though research can provide lists of words from children's vocabularies for incorporation in initial reading schemes there are still many problems— whether to use writing or speaking vocabulary; the time lag between research and incorporation in reading materials which may result in an already dated vocabulary being utilised; the extent to which vocabulary is 'area' or- child-specific. Awareness of the problems highlighted particularly by the difficulties of 'deprived' and immigrant children whose language experience may be so atypical, led some teachers to develop their own reading materials based on the vocabulary of their particular children. Others have used programmed techniques based on 'linguistic' principles in which the child responds not by oral reading but by written letters and words, self-checking of the responses being provided. Here the story books may be supplementary rather than basic. When the child is 'reading' from the story books his techniques are therefore more similar to fluent adult reading at that level of difficulty than is possible when the reading books are the basis of instruction.

Attention has now been turned to the language structure in early reading books rather than to the vocabulary control. In the early books of many popular reading schemes the 'sentences' are in reality only a structure into which to slot the necessary frequent repetitions of the basic sight vocabulary. Many of the books can be faulted because of their unnecessarily limited sentence structure which makes the stories less interesting than they need have been, even within the constraints of the vocabulary control. Recently research has shown the range of sentence structures used in the spoken language of pre-school children and evidence of appreciation of a wide range of grammatical structures even by so-called 'deprived' children. What is a matter of still greater concern, however, in the '*un-English*' structure of the stilted sentences is their unpredictability which prevents the child from developing appropriate strategies for detecting the sequential probability in linguistic structure. In short, such materials are not merely limited but also deficient. The importance of syntax in early reading materials is now being appreciated as evidence is appearing that children while learning to read can make use of their implicit knowledge of grammar. Studies of differential error patterns in children taught by a range of approaches and with different types of materials would yield interesting information on this aspect.

There has been considerable emphasis on the importance of both teachers and parents reading aloud to children as a preparation for early reading experiences. The focus has, however, been on the motivational values of such attention by parents. Reid [1972] has, however, drawn attention to the possibility that reading aloud may have specific values in the pre-reading and early reading stages in familiarising the child with orally presented *written* linguistic structures. Such experience may well accelerate a child's reading progress in the early stages if appropriate reading materials are then employed. Experimental studies with pre-school children and school beginners to investigate the effects on reading progress of *story telling* or *story reading* and the effects of different types of orally presented reading materials would be relevant here. It may be that oral reading by the teacher to the children in her class, or of one child to another, should be an integral part of the reading instruction in order to develop in the listener the appropriate techniques for fluent reading. Oral reading continued with children with limited reading or language fluency may be an important part of their language development. Information, appreciation and relaxation are certainly three purposes in oral reading by the teacher, but development of an intuitive awareness of written linguistic structures may also be important. Here also the contribution to the development of linguistic competence provided by parents who provide their children with a range of orally presented reading materials may not have been fully appreciated. The effects of home background on motivation and receptivity to the school's instruction has been stressed rather more. It may be that deficiency in language teaching in the schools is less apparent because of the contribution of parents. In this instance parents may have been compensating for the deficiencies of the school.

The Schools Council Research Project which led to the publication of *Breakthrough to Literacy* is an example of an initial reading programme based on language generated by the children themselves. The initial reading materials are sentences produced by the child and recorded with the aid of the 'sentence maker'. Basic word cards are provided and others can be supplied by the teacher as required. The children progress until they are able to produce their own words on the 'word maker'. The language used is that generated by teacher and/or child and it is argued in the manual[15] that where children are actively involved in this way, frequent repetition of words is not necessarily required before children remember them. The books in this project are based on vocabulary, interests, and language generated by the children in the research project. The basic materials provided in the 'Breakthrough' kit and the reading books will not, however, determine how the materials are used, nor indeed will the information in the manual lead to any uniformity of presentation. Teachers adopting 'Breakthrough' whose initial approach is that of a 'counsellor' as defined by Southgate and Roberts[16] and who are already using the children's oral language as the basis for the initial reading experiences may be led to a more structured and progressively organised awareness of the rate and nature of development of the individual children. The teacher 'instructor' used to an initial approach based on a reading scheme as the structure for a planned approach may on adopting 'Breakthrough' develop an equally successful but very different technique for utilising the materials. An interesting and relevant piece of research would be a study of the differential in the approaches to the teaching of reading and the various integral parts of *Breakthrough* by competent, experienced teachers with basically different views on the role of the teacher in the instructor–counsellor continuum.

Adoption of a scheme such as *Breakthrough* with a basis in the language and experience of the children will not provide more than a framework for the development of a language approach to the teaching of reading.

Not only will limitations in the language of the children affect their progress with approaches such as *Breakthrough to Literacy* unless active steps are taken to develop their oral language and their appreciation of the powers of written communication, but the limitations in the teacher's own language and her capacity to arouse, stimulate and extend the language of the children will be crucial. Attention has been centred on the deficiencies of the child in the learning situation and the inadequacies of the parents. To quote Bernstein:[17]

> The compensatory education concept serves to direct attention away from the internal organisation and the education context of the school, and focus our attention upon the families and children. Compensatory education implies that something is lacking in the family, and so in the child, and that as a result the children are unable to benefit from schools (pp. 53–4). . . . we should stop thinking in terms of compensatory education but consider instead most seriously and systematically the conditions and contexts of the educational environment.(p. 55)

It is important to appreciate that even 'language-deprived' children from 'inadequate' homes have probably been bombarded with speech and that their deficiency is not, except in very rare instances, as a result of lack of experience of spoken language. In many such homes television provides an almost continuous additional pattern of speech. Recent studies have also shown that pre-school children, even those whose language performance is limited, have in most instances acquired an appreciation of a wider range of linguistic structures than was previously appreciated. Thus two of the emphases in some programmes for 'deprived' children—(i) ample experiences of language and (ii) models of grammatical structures for them to reproduce, are perhaps misplaced. The crucial features seem to be experiences in attempts to communicate using language with a range of recipients in a variety of situations. These children need to learn how to explain, and what to ask in order to receive further appropriate information. Studies on the effect of particular language situations on the quality and quantity of language produced by children are relevant here. The work of Donaldson and her co-workers in Edinburgh[18] has indicated the effects on language production of the specific types of situation employed, while Kamii[19] has devised with pre-school children programmes for developing and testing their cognitive abilities which are less dependent on the limited language which the children may possess for expressing their solutions. Situation variables and their influence on spontaneity, length and complexity, style and content of language are discussed by Cazden under the heading of 'The neglected situation in child language, research and education'.[20] She considers the relevance of the topic, the task, and the listener to the quantity and complexity of language elicited. Clearly it is important in developing language programmes within an educational context, whether oral or written, that research information is available and is used so that the language experiences provided and the responses elicited are planned systematically and sequentially to meet the needs of the individual child. Previous emphasis on deprivation, and a need for models of speech, has perhaps focused the educational needs in language terms on too limited and even on inappropriate aspects. Blank[21] in the same volume *Language and Poverty* (p. 71) claims that:

> Psycholinguists, like behaviourists provide an extremely limited empirical basis from which to derive guidelines for teaching language skills to children, whether disadvantaged or otherwise. The result has been that in the teaching of verbal abilities there has been an orientation similar to that in overall enrichment; namely try to offer every possible language skill that may be important.

She feels there are major problems in teaching 'higher-level cognition' in a group setting except to children whose home has already provided and is providing a 'rich one-to-one verbal interchange'. In a group setting attention is diluted and sporadic and therefore will not provide the child with the essential stimulus and feed-back. Blank, like others, sees the learning difficulties of many children as 'reflecting the children's failure to develop a symbolic system which would permit them to see the plentiful stimulation already available to them, as existing in a coherent, logical and predictable framework' (p. 73). This is as significant to learning to read as it is to oral language development.

Clearly, therefore, the task of language stimulation and development is complex and the provision of materials for the recording of the language as in 'Breakthrough' will not in itself provide an adequate language-based approach to learning to read. The solution will not be in additional pre-packed language programmes, even if developed from researches into the efficacy of different approaches to language teaching. A programme planned for certain children in a particular situation will not transfer unmodified to other children in a different setting. Such studies could, however, assist teachers in planning their own developmental language programmes of which reading would be an integral part. In *Talk Reform* D. M. and J. A. Gahagan[22] describe the development of a variety of language experiences within the research project by research workers and teachers together. The aim of the programme was to broaden the active language experience of the children and to sensitise them to the variety of language structures so that they would appreciate the appropriateness of particular structures for specific situations. Participation in such a study could sensitise not only the children, but also the teachers involved in the programme to a greater awareness of the needs and potential of their children. The subsequent provision of language kits for other teachers would, however, in no way replicate the situation and would possibly be as inappropriate as the technique it might replace where the children had been the passive recipients of the teacher's language, varied and stimulating though it might have been.

Further investigation is required into the qualities and skills which characterise the successful language teacher so that as far as possible these skills can be developed by the training programmes in colleges. It is important to analyse the extent to which the teacher's own language is an important variable in the situation. Is there a 'deprived teacher' syndrome? Is this a significant factor in children's failures and could language enrichment programmes in colleges enrich and sensitise the teachers? What else is required by the teacher to be successful in the type of rôle she is now expected to fulfil? There is evidence from a variety of studies that the teaching of grammar even by a direct approach does not assist the development of children's written compositions. It is also possible that the teaching of linguistics to teachers in training may have disappointingly little effect on their teaching performance. Many student teachers may be no more ready or able to grasp the significance of linguistics than school children the rules of grammar. To quote Morris' eponymous dictum, 'You Can't Teach What You Don't Know'.[23] The crucial question is, however, *What* must a teacher know? Here also research is needed into the extent to which, and the ways in which, teachers are influenced by different content and presentation within their own training programme.

We in education are too ready to accept the successes and ascribe the failures to the parents. Brandis and Henderson[24] studied mothers' communications with their children at the pre-school stage and then studied the children during their first three years in school. They found that the social classes differed radically in their use of language for purposes of explanation and control and in the willingness of the mothers to respond to communications which their children initiated. An equally important finding, however, was the predictive value of an index of maternal communication *within* social class and for children of the same measured level of ability as measured by intelligence tests. There is need for more sophisticated and precise information on the extent to which maternal and paternal communication contributes to children's educational success and the ways in which it does and could interact with the language environment in the school. We have no opportunity of knowing how children from favoured home backgrounds would develop with regard to reading and related skills after the age of five without the intervention of formalised educational institutions. It is important that we analyse the extent to which, within social class, and at comparable levels of intelligence on initial testing at five years of age, the educational success of the child is influenced by the *language* environment of the home. There is an attitude in the teaching profession and among educationists in general that the education in school provides the material and the stimulus, and that the rôle of the parent is to prepare the child to be ready and willing to receive the instruction—the concepts of *readiness for school* and *reading readiness* exemplifying this outlook. In my present research on fluent readers the embarrassment of a number of the parents at sending their child to school already reading fluently is distressing. Ready but not too ready seems to be the keynote. Once the child commences school, the rôle of the parent is seen by many as providing 'interest', 'acceptance', and 'appreciation'. The language environment which the home provides may be the crucial variable in the success in reading and related skills of some children, particularly if reading is assessed as a language process. When evaluating the

factors influencing success in reading we may be drawing erroneous conclusions if we concentrate specifically on the school
environment; home variables must also be considered, particularly
language interaction. The contributions of the home to the learning situation should be measured in more sophisticated terms than
numbers of visits to the school, number of books in the home, socioeconomic class, etc. Significant information might be obtained
from studying the strategies in language tuition of 'successful'
parents—a little-tapped field of enquiry. The planned increase in
nursery education will, it has been claimed, make children better
able to benefit from primary education. Here, no less than elsewhere in education, will it be insufficient to provide a rich environment in language terms, and assume children will benefit.
There *are* dangers in the possible implications that parents do not
or cannot provide the necessary language stimulation for their
children. Some do and many more could. It is equally important
in pre-school and in-school education that objectives are defined;
that techniques are evolved for achieving these, and that appropriate instruments are devised which will enable the success of
the teaching to be evaluated.

One major weakness in the teaching of language and reading
generally is that objectives are not being specifically defined in
behavioural terms and success cannot therefore be effectively
measured. The existing reading tests are no more adequate as
measures of the range of skills involved in fluent reading than are
the language tests used in pre-school evaluation adequate as
measures of the language performance of children. It is important
that more sensitive and sophisticated measures be utilised in research projects into both oral language and reading progress,
otherwise the weaknesses and the strengths of the children and of
the teaching techniques will not be effectively analysed. An essential
prerequisite in any attempts to devise adequate tests of reading
is an evaluation of the skills displayed by the fluent reader and ways
of translating these into behavioural objectives together with an
analysis of the extent to which any such 'reading efficiencies'[25]
are composed of distinguishable sub-skills. Essential also to the
development of appropriate testing instruments for the evaluation
of the learning at different stages in the process towards adult
literate reading would be an analysis of the learning process
in reading. Particular attention should be paid to whether the
learning necessitates a sequential progression through a hierarchy
of sub-skills to the final achievement of higher-order skills. It

may be that some of these steps are merely hurdles—or barriers—interspersed as a result of the types of approach to the teaching of reading employed in the schools. It is hoped that the present writer's study of children who learned to read fluently outside the school-group situation may throw some light on this question. In this, as in many of the other aspects of research into language and reading mentioned during this paper an interdisciplinary approach involving linguists and psychologists should add an important dimension.

The result may be:

A clearer understanding of what the skilled reader can do and of what the beginning reader is trying to do, [which] is far more important for the reading teacher than any revision of instructional materials.[26]

NOTES

1. Start, K. B., and Wells, B. K., *The Trend of Reading Standards*, National Foundation for Educational Research in England and Wales, Slough 1972.
2. Cf. Downing, J., and Thackray, D. V., *Reading Readiness*, University of London Press Ltd., London 1971.
3. See Wyman, J. M., 'Auditory discrimination, speech and reading', in *The Elementary School Journal*, **60,** 1960, pp. 325–33; Clark, M. M., *Reading Difficulties in Schools*, Penguin Papers in Education, Penguin, Harmondsworth 1970.
4. Hardy, M. I., 'The development of beginning reading skills: recent findings', in M. M. Clark and A. Milne (eds.), *Reading and Related Skills*, Ward Lock Educational, London, in press.
5. Wilkinson, A., *The Foundations of Language*, Oxford University Press, London 1971.
6. Cf. Fry, D. B., 'Speech reception and perception', in J. Lyons (ed.), *New Horizons in Linguistics*, Penguin, Harmondsworth 1970, pp. 29–52.
7. Clark, M. M., *Reading: The Patterning of Complex Behaviour*, Heinemann Educational Books, Auckland 1972; and *The Early Detection of Reading Difficulties—A Diagnostic Survey*, Heinemann Educational Books, Auckland 1972.
8. Merritt, J. E., 'The intermediate skills: towards a better understanding of the process of fluent reading'. First published in K. W. Gardner (ed.), *Reading Skills: Theory and Practice*, Ward Lock Educational, London 1970. Subsequently reprinted in J. M.

Morris (ed.), *The First R: Yesterday, Today and Tomorrow*, Ward Lock Educational, London 1972.

9. Smith, F., *Understanding Reading*, Holt, Rinehart & Winston, New York 1971.

10. Goodman, K. S., 'Reading: a psycholinguistic guessing game', in H. Singer and R. B. Ruddell (eds.), *Theoretical Models and Processes of Reading*, International Reading Association, Newark, Delaware 1970.

11. Reid, J. F., 'Learning to think about reading', *Educational Research*, **9**, 1960, pp. 56–62.

12. Downing, J., 'How children think about reading', *The Reading Teacher*, **23**, iii, 1969, pp. 217–30.

13. Hardy, M. I., 'The development of beginning reading skills: recent findings', in M. M. Clark and A. Milne (eds.), *Reading and Related Skills*, Ward Lock Educational, London, in press.

14. Reid, J. F., 'Children's comprehension of syntactic features found in some extension readers', in J. F. Reid (ed.), *Reading Problems and Practices*, Ward Lock Educational, London 1972, pp. 394–403.

15. Mackay, D., Thompson, B., and Schaub, P., *Breakthrough to Literacy*, Teacher's Manual, Longman, London 1970.

16. Southgate, V., and Roberts, J. R., *Reading—which approach?*, University of London Press, London 1970.

17. Bernstein, B., 'A sociolinguistic approach to socialisation: with some references to educability', in F. Williams (ed.), *Language and Poverty*, Markham Press, Chicago 1970.

18. See Campbell, R., and Wales, R., 'The study of language acquisition', in J. Lyons (ed.), *New Horizons in Linguistics*, Penguin, Harmondsworth 1970.

19. Kamii, C., 'Evaluation of learning in pre-school education: socio-emotional, perceptual-motor, cognitive development', in B. S. Bloom, J. T. Hastings and G. F. Madaus (eds.) *Handbook on Formative and Summative Evaluation of Student Learning*, McGraw-Hill, New York 1971, pp. 281–344.

20. In F. Williams (ed.), *Language and Poverty*, Markham Publ. Co., Chicago 1970.

21. Ibid.

22. Gagahan, D. M., and Gagahan, G. A., *Talk Reform: Exploration in Language for Infant Children*, Routledge & Kegan Paul, London 1970.

23. In M. M. Clark and A. Milne (eds.), *Reading and Related Skills*, Ward Lock Educational, London, in press.

24. Brandis, W., and Henderson, D., *Social Class, Language and Communication*, Routledge & Kegan Paul, London 1970.

25. Gatherer, W. A., 'Extending reading efficiencies', in M. M. Clark and A. Milne (eds.), op. cit. (see above, n. 23).

26. Smith, F., op. cit. (n. 9 above), p. 230.

SPEAKER'S INTRODUCTION

I want to focus on specific points in my paper in an attempt to high-light what seems to me particularly significant from a research point of view. In my view psychologists have too often focused on the negative aspects of reading and of the teaching of reading, and perhaps by so doing have stressed as crucial areas which are not so.

1. I think studies of reading readiness need to look at children who learn to read successfully in different circumstances and by different strategies. Studies of reading readiness need, of course, to be followed through by studies of reading behaviour—and here I think studies like Marie Clay's on errors are particularly useful.

2. I wonder to what extent some children have difficulties in reading which are caused not by the nature of the reading task in itself but by the language of *instruction* used by the teacher.

3. There has been a good deal of emphasis on the importance of children being read to before they start school. This is fine, but I think the related aspect would repay interest, i.e. a comparison between story-telling and the reaction of the child to story-reading. This relates, of course, to the well-attested difference between spoken and written patterns and also to the demarcation by e.g. Reid[1] and Downing[2] that children may have problems with the language structure of early read-ing books. I am therefore advocating here a move towards the teaching of reading as a linguistic guessing game.

4. We need to know more about the use by different teachers of the *same* materials. I cannot accept that language kits will achieve what might have been expected of them when teachers have such different approaches, and some exhibit considerable poverty of language.

5. We need to know more about the interaction between the 'good' home and the 'good' school. It may be, after all, that the home is crucial, not in the sense of stimulating the child to learn to read in school but in the sense of actually causing him to do so through the language interaction in the home.

6. More important than national surveys, it seems to me, are attempts to decide on the objectives that we are trying to achieve in reading, and attempts to devise tests to measure these objectives.

Within several of the areas of enquiry that I have mentioned research projects bringing together a range of different disciplines would surely achieve much more useful results than if the studies had been done by one discipline only. This would prevent the determining of the problem and therefore of the range of possible solutions that we were warned against in the preceding paper.

NOTES

1. Reid, J. F., 'Children's comprehension of syntactic features found in some extension readers', in J. F. Reid (ed.), *Reading Problems and Practices*, Ward Lock Educational, London 1972, pp. 394–403.
2. Downing, J., 'How children think about reading', *The Reading Teacher*, **23**, iii, 1969, pp. 217–30.

Discussant: *John E. Merritt*

Margaret Clark has presented her views on so many important aspects of reading with such economy that it is only possible, in the time available, to present a few impressionistic comments. There are no fundamental points on which I would take issue with Clark except, perhaps, in matters of emphasis, so my own comments consist of riders with which Clark may or may not entirely agree. I will comment on reading readiness and early reading, the development of intermediate skills and comprehension, and, in passing, on one or two of the implications for teachers and for parents.

Reading Readiness and Early Reading

Clark has pointed to certain deficiencies in tests of reading readiness and to the misleading nature of the information they provide. I would like to go further and question the value of the term 'reading readiness' itself. My reason for challenging the term is that it is so often taken to imply that readiness comes at some particular point of time. Very often, perhaps, it is used to refer to the time when a child is thought to be ready to read the first book in some reading scheme or other. But there are many skills that are specific to reading that must be acquired before a child can profitably be exposed to a book which he is expected to learn to read. For example, he must acquire certain learning sets. He must acquire a 'set' to scan words from left to right, to attend to the orientation of otherwise identical letters (p–b–d–q; n–u; t–f, and, perhaps, h–y and m–w). Before this, he must acquire a 'set' to attend to letter shape and ignore such variables as colour, size, thickness of line, etc. There are sets to be established concerning relationships between letters, groups of letters, and words, and the sounds, sound-sequences and meanings which they represent. The specific learnings and the generalised learning sets to be acquired are, in fact, many and varied. There is no single point at which all of these skills and learning sets can be deemed to be acquired and a state of readiness attained. Rather, there is, or should be, a steady acquisition of basic sub-skills on which more advanced skills are successively built during the school years. For this reason, I would suggest that the term 'reading readiness' has served its purpose. The crude concept of developmental stages must now give way, I would suggest, to a concept of continuous development in a variety of related areas. We can then concentrate systematically on achieving steady progress in terms of each child's developmental profile instead of merely providing activities of a very general kind and waiting for 'readiness' to arrive as a result of some sort of spontaneous manifestation.

It is easy to understand how the idea has developed that readiness can best be fostered by providing a 'rich educational experience'. This, after all, is the best condition for fostering the development of language. Unfortunately, however, reading is different from language in many important respects, even though it is basically dependent on language. Language is used automatically in dealing with children in a variety of situations, and this exposure to language in various forms is a necessary (but not sufficient) condition for language acquisition. In addition, the child's own language is a powerful tool which can be used in a large number of situations to manipulate others. Thus there is a continuously high level of motivation for the child to use language in whatever way is most effective in a given situation. Neither of these conditions exists in the case of reading. We can only approximate to these conditions by designing a large number of items for teaching the sub-skills of reading in the early years. These must go as far as possible towards providing the kind of exposure to reading that children get in the case of language and a degree of motivation of the same order. Even the best design will not get us to those targets, of course. But, it is hoped, a professional approach to design should take us well beyond the present standard of provision.

Materials for developing the early skills should provide a high degree of intrinsic motivation. But in saying this we must remember Clark's caution that they must also be designed in such a way that they permit, rather than interfere with, a ready transfer of learning. They should also be self-correcting—bad habits learned at this stage may have a critical influence on later development, and so correction must be immediate. They should not, in my view, form part of a structured programme. Rather, they should be available on demand. A child will not play with material that is too difficult and will soon tire of material that is too easy. To a large extent, therefore, the child can programme his own development if suitable materials are available.

Materials of the kind I am proposing must, of course, be available in the home. They must not, however, be used for direct instruction. Once this happens their motivation value is all too often destroyed. If the parent needs to teach the child anything more than the rudiments of how to handle the material, the material is not adequately designed for the job it has to do.

Basically, then, what I am suggesting is that we need a much more rigorous attack on the design of materials for early reading—but we need to have due regard for the 'conventional wisdom' of the progressive infant teacher in deciding how it should be used.

Before leaving the question of the design of materials and methods for teaching reading in the early stages, I wonder if I might add to the points made by Clark a comment on 'mixed methods'. It is often affirmed that teachers who adopt 'mixed methods' are 'getting the best of both worlds'. How much more often, I wonder, would it be more accurate to talk of 'falling between two stools'. The two stools, needless to say, are 'phonics' and 'look-and-say'. This is not to say that I disapprove of mixed methods. But unfortunately, much of the teaching of phonics consists of teaching rules which are promptly contradicted by the next few words the child reads in a 'look-and-say' primer. A psychologist could not design a better situation for producing experimental neurosis. I have no doubt that it is precisely this condition that accounts for the failure of a significant number of children to cope with the early stages of reading.[1] Happily, there is some evidence[2] which suggests that experimental neurosis is much less likely to develop in a supportive environment. This, no doubt, is why some teachers are so successful in teaching reading in spite of the difficulties presented by the irregularities of the orthography—and in spite of the fact that their methods may often leave something to be desired.

The Intermediate Skills

Clark made reference to what I have spoken of elsewhere as 'intermediate skills'.[3] These are the skills involved when we use context cues to anticipate what is to follow in a text. We may anticipate a letter or a sound (balloo–), a word (The bus stopped at the bus . . .), or, more generally, a meaning (I know those people—they are all ——). And, of course, we anticipate the related syntactic features. In recent years it has become increasingly clear that our ability to recognise in a running text words that are not in our spoken vocabulary is highly dependent upon our ability to respond to context cues, i.e., to transitional probabilities, and that this ability is also of the greatest importance in fluent reading. Now, however, there is a tendency in some quarters to place such value on anticipated meanings that the actual words in the text are effectively devalued. Thus, followers of Goodman may, for example, accept the word 'supper' in oral reading when the text says 'dinner'. Now I have been stressing the importance of responding to transitional probabilities for some years. I would be seriously concerned, however, if teachers now started to undervalue the importance of accurate word perception. If we do not encourage children both to anticipate meanings *and* to perceive words accurately we shall simply be encouraging incompetent reading. And then, no doubt, we shall get a pendulum swing back to phonics and structural word attack. I would suggest, therefore, that we accept the importance of using both approaches simultaneously, rather than adopt an 'either-or' position.

Comprehension

In talking about language development Clark pointed out that the emphases in some programmes for deprived children are perhaps misplaced. She suggested that 'the crucial features in language programmes seem to be experiences in attempts to communicate using language with a range of recipients in a variety of situations.' I would simply like to emphasise that this holds for written language as much as it does for spoken language. One of the least useful things teachers can do to children is to ask them to write screeds of material during the school years merely to obtain marks for the record card. One of the most useful things teachers can do is to ensure that as much as possible of what is written is written for the purpose of communicating it to someone else. The writing may be expressive, or transactional. It may be a poem or a short story, a report of a field study or an experiment. Whatever the kind of writing the quality will be improved, I suggest, when there is a genuine need or desire to communicate. If the need to receive the communication is equally strong, then that, I suggest, provides the best possible basis for the development of comprehension. This means, of course, that we must put the curriculum first and language and reading second, for this is where the need to communicate must originate. In saying this I am not intending to suggest that language and reading should not be accorded a high degree of priority in education. What I would say is that if we change the curriculum so that it has some chance of achieving the high-minded educational aims we all tend to subscribe to we shall automatically provide conditions that are conducive to the development of language and reading. Teachers, however, would need a far better training than they receive at present in order to take advantage of the opportunities thus offered. In order to achieve this I suggest that we must place the teachers in learning situations similar to those that we regard as suitable for the children they are to teach. This way they may begin to see how theory can be put to work.

Clark made some valuable comments on the importance of the parent in relation to the child's development of language and of reading. I should simply like to add that the parent, too, would benefit by being given experiences similar to the children's. A number of schools in this country and the United States have invited parents to engage in this kind of activity. I think this is a valuable field for action research. Perhaps, however, we should be doing very much more in the schools to provide children with opportunities for learning parental rôles instead of waiting until they are actually parents. By then, the damage is already done.

NOTES

1. See Merritt, J. E., 'The intermediate skills: towards a better understanding of the process of fluent reading'. First published in K. W.

Gardner (ed.), *Reading skills: Theory and Practice*, Ward Lock Educational, London 1970. Subsequently reprinted in J. M. Morris (ed.), *The First R: Yesterday, Today* and *Tomorrow*, Ward Lock Educational, London 1972.

2. See, e.g., Liddell, 1954
3. See n.1, above.

GENERAL DISCUSSION

K. Dougall The relationship between teacher and child is a very special one, in which the teacher accepts each child, is aware of his abilities and optimistic about his future. The child, for his part, accepts the teacher as someone he knows is on his side. This relationship allows a certain relaxing of the pressure of having to reach a certain level of attainment by a certain age. Teacher and child are involved together in the task of learning to read.

Jessie Reid I should like to link this with a different point, namely the study of errors. I was interested in Clark's remarks about the importance of such a study. May I make two branching points here. One is the use of errors in helping us study the process of the acquisition of literacy as an intellectual feat. The other relates to what Bruner said in his paper about there being many different roads to a solution. Looking at errors is a very important way of trying to decide what different individuals are in fact doing. And this can be a contribution to the theoretical study of what it is to become literate.

Marie Clay My own work and that of people like Goodman[1] has produced evidence that may be running counter to the current stress on the value of semantics. This evidence indicates that the child in the very early stages of reading predicts the kind of word that will fit in with the structure more frequently, even when it is an error, than he predicts something which belongs to the same semantic field. Gradually, over the first few years of instruction, the errors tend to have the same visual form; many of the letters are the ones in the original text. They still have a syntactic equivalence but they are coming to have a very close semantic link too. Errors still occur but by now they indicate that children are looking for all three types of cue. Of course these results may have come from an analysis that has used a structural approach; on the other hand we may be right and this is a characteristic of the learning-to-read process.

Halliday I find that point very interesting. May I suggest that part of the reason for this finding may be the fact that a child has not yet at that early stage interpreted the reading operation as a linguistic one. In other words, he is not expecting it to produce meaning; and I think it is time to say that in a large amount of reading experience the child is decoding only at the structural level because he has not slotted it into his own language experience. Now may I go on from this to ride my hobby-horse on the functional approach. I wonder if Clark would agree that we know very little about where reading experience fits into the child's functional experience with language? In terms of the development of the human race there came a moment when it became necessary to adopt a new meaning for the language. New functions evolved for language which could not be satisfied by the spoken medium. The human race evolved writing. Once again, then, we can see how the development of the child matches—up to a point—that of the species. In functional terms I would say that reading comes to make sense as a necessary activity for the child when he sees how reading—and only reading—can open up new horizons for him. This is the only way, I think, in which reading readiness makes any sense.

I am not so happy with Merritt's formulation of reading as an absolutely artificial operation as contrasted with the natural activity of speaking. I do not like this division because relatively speaking I think there is no discontinuity. I think it is essential to interpret the use of the written medium as a natural extension of language in the spoken medium.

Davies Just as we do not normally speak of the child's learning to speak as making errors, so perhaps we should stress—as Dougall has reminded us—the importance of the teacher–child cooperation in learning to read. A successful cooperation of that sort must have a lot in common with the mother–child relation in learning to speak. All approximations in school to reading should be considered as successful approximations.

Britton Whatever needs or functions arose that caused the human race to invent writing I think we need to look at a different set of functions that give the necessary motivation to children to learn to read. I think children learn to read because they want to read stories. A four-year-old son of a friend of mine was recently dictating a story to his mother, and one of the sentences was, 'The prince went sadly home, for he had nowhere else to go.' Obviously 'for he had nowhere else to go' was not something he had drawn from his speech; he had internalised written forms by listening to stories his mother read to him. He is already *in* the other language before going to school. We have not yet looked very much at the child's motivation to make this other language his own.

Gatherer I must say that in spite of Halliday's parallel between human and child development and Merritt's advice about children being given a parental rôle, I still think the home is a crucial influence in stimulating the child's learning. Parents should be *encouraged* to take more interest in their children's language. I would like to ask Clark to tell us more about her work with gifted children.

Margaret Clark   When I mentioned fluent readers I was not necessarily talking about gifted children, and I think that this is the interesting part of this study. These children came from all kinds of homes—what they have in common seems to be that their parents provide a very rich language environment.

I agree with the comment that too much stress has been placed on oral reading. We need it in order to specify errors but we do not need to make children *learn* to read orally. I have asked the mothers of these fluent readers, 'When did you know he could read?' Several have replied, 'I didn't realise for a while, and then he asked me what that word was. I wondered why he asked about *that* one and then I realised he knew all the others.'

I am not very happy about more sophisticated analyses of text difficulty. It is too difficult, I think, to detach the level of text difficulty from the child, his background, motivation and expectation.

Merritt   In terms of the analysis of error I should like to mention the work done by Jahoda and L. Thomas.[2] They have avoided the emphasis on word attack skills that such studies tend to make by their use of a reading recorder to see at what rate people process texts. They are, in fact, enabling the reader to go straight for meaning, and then analysing his route. It is meaning that all readers should be helped toward from the start—word attack skills will improve anyway.

I should like to see reading become much more of a cooperative activity; every specialist and teacher should be made aware that it is her job to help children become self-organised as readers. This means putting children in situations where they will discuss with each other the meanings in the text. It is also helpful, I suggest, to give children every opportunity for comparative reading, using, for example, textbooks giving different accounts of the same historical period. We need to start both at the meaning end and at the skills end.

Bernstein   There seem to be two aspects to this problem. One is that you apply certain means in order to get certain outcomes. The other has to do with those means, with the theory on which they rest. When a certain means is used to transmit something, what the child experiences is also something else; those sets of social relationships bound up in the means. You may say that you are using certain means to make the child self-regulating; but the kind of self-regulation the child achieves inheres in the deep structure of the means you have used.

Other points were made in the discussion by:
H. Nathan
J. S. Bruner

NOTES

1. Goodman, K. S., 'Reading: a psycholinguistic guessing game', in H. Singer and R. B. Ruddell (eds.), *Theoretical Models and Processes of Reading*, International Reading Association, Newark, Delaware 1970.
2. Jahoda, Marie and Thomas Laurie, 'The Mechanics of Learning', *New Scientist* 14 April 1966, pp. 114–17.

5

Teaching Writing

JAMES BRITTON

There is no use indicting words, they are no shoddier than what they peddle.

SAMUEL BECKETT[1]

The practical and theoretical importance of the problems raised by studying the process of writing are, I think, obvious. Most people, whether they write often or seldom, admit to finding the task difficult, though a number would add that they enjoy it once they have got into their stride. And to pursue that practical problem leads us, I hope to show, into some matters of basic theoretical interest.

The Medium

There seems to have been very little study of the effect of the medium upon the process. The 9-year-old who writes a ten-page story is not uncommon in today's primary schools, though clearly this could not have happened when a slate and a pencil were the only materials provided.

Drafting *by hand*, on a *typewriter* or by *dictation* must represent three differing effects upon what is drafted, though the differences may be ironed out when the writing process culminates in a *reading* of what has been drafted to arrive at the final version. There are people, however, who do very little to the draft produced by a typist from their dictation and in my experience this seems to result (for reasons I do not fully understand) in writing that I can only call tedious. D. W. Harding has claimed that 'a great deal of speaking and writing involves the effort to be a little more faithful to the non-verbal background of language than an over-ready acceptance of ready-made terms and phrases will permit.'[2] Perhaps the effort takes two respective forms: interactional effects in speech, and, in writing, the full exploitation of the possibilities of re-drafting. 'Dictation on to the page' makes use of neither form.

A fourth category of medium needs to be noted, namely modes of writing which exploit visually two-dimensional space. Recent interest in a theory of graphic communication may hasten the development of new modes which might affect writing quite substantially. Henry R. Cassirer, UNESCO Director of the Division of Use of Mass Media, has claimed that visual communication 'is a language in its own right'; by which he appears to mean that it 'stands on its own as a means of conceptualisation expression and communication'.[3] We are already familiar with 'concrete poetry', with two-tailed poems (cf. Coleridge's marginal annotations as an integral part of *The Ancient Mariner*), and with a diversity of ways in which the techniques of advertising are encroaching onto the layout of the text in journalism.

The Physical Setting

Again, very little study has been made of the physical setting in which writing takes place, and what little there has suggests that individuals vary so much as to what circumstances are favourable to the activity that findings would probably be of limited value.[4] Nevertheless, where writing is demanded in a prearranged situation (notably the examination room) we ought to be in a better position than we are to make the most suitable arrangements.

The Process: Premeditation:

The fact that in writing we utter here and now to be heard elsewhere and later on has often enough been remarked upon and implications drawn. We may, for example, construct in imagination the situations in which our writing will be read, and whether we do this or not, we certainly address ourselves to 'an internalised other' in some form. Comparing the writer's with the speaker's behaviour, we may regard these efforts as a means of supplying our own feedback: and go on to note that at least we have time given to us to do this (subject of course to other conditions).

This amounts to noting that writing is a premeditated utterance; but we need to know a great deal more about the various ways in which various people, engaged on various tasks, make use of this time for premeditation. Do writers sometimes use it to hammer out an utterance with a deliberation quite unlike the way speech is generated? Or is a speech-like 'flow' an essential stage in producing writing, and the time then spent either in trying out

one 'spurt', rejecting it and trying another, or in making detailed
alterations to the draft that a spurt has produced?

Continuity in Utterance

In the London Association for the Teaching of English some years
ago[5] we devised a reading comprehension test and, in the course
of trying it out, examined its correlates within a battery containing
(1) a vocabulary test based on the text of the comprehension
test; (2) the Mill Hill vocabulary test; (3) a Moray House non-
verbal and (4) an NFER verbal intelligence test; (5) a reading-
speed test, and (6) a piece of free writing. The trio that best pre-
dicted the comprehension scores was a combination of the
verbal IQ test, the Mill Hill Vocabulary test and the free writing
(multiple correlation .77), and the variance was distributed as
follows: free writing 27.8%, vocab. test 22.3%, IQ test 8.7%.
Free writing and reading comprehension were the only tests in
the battery that consisted in the handling of continuous language:
this factor appeared to outweigh the differences between language
production and reception. Is continuous language, whether we
read it or speak it or write it, something of a vortex into which the
mind is drawn?

The Writing Research team experimented with carrying out a
writing task without being able to read what was written—both
by hand and on a typewriter. We sensed no great difficulty in
writing a letter (to a member of the team who conveniently
happened to be in America), some handicap in trying to write a
story, and considerable frustration in writing a research report. Our
recorded writings when we read them lent support to our feelings.

Systematic studies along these lines, and investigations of planned interruptions to writing, and other artificial 'noise' effects,
might secure some evidence as to how writers employ the gap
between utterance and reception, or (more strictly) between
first drafting and the finished product.

The rôle of planning in writing is obviously another aspect of
this same problem. If continuity is an important feature of
language, if 'flow' is an appropriate way of thinking of language
production, then over-planning is likely to be a greater danger than
under-planning. Many writers say, for example, that they recover
from interruptions by reading the last 'run' of what they have
written and then writing on. We certainly found the inability to
do this one of the main difficulties in trying to write without
being able to see what we had written. That this should be the case

is by no means as inevitable as it may seem at first sight. Why should we jump on the bus of our own prior activity rather than read, pause and say, 'Here I am, now where shall I go next?' It may well be that shaping at the point of utterance is as important in writing as it is in conversation, that the linguistic flow generates our movements towards the next objective. However, we need a lot more evidence before we can be sure.

The point is of pedagogical importance of course: perhaps the usual teacher's insistence on planning, on 'thinking before you write', is mistaken, or at least mistaken with regard to some kinds of plan and some kinds of writing task. It has more fundamental importance also as an existing gap in our understanding of intellectual processes.

Individual drafting processes remain something of a mystery, then. Differences in prior speech experience must affect them, and James Moffett,[6] among others, has suggested the planning of speech activities in school as an approach to writing. Peter Wason[7] finds it necessary at some stage in drafting to externalise his 'internalised other' in the person of a colleague, and most of us probably do something of the sort in a rather less systematic way. Less systematic because, in many kinds of writing, the author's point of view as a whole comes over in subtle and non-deliberate ways which (while it might be profitable to exchange the author's viewpoint for another writer's) are lost when one writer takes over another's emendations. Topic headings and other jottings, extended charts or lay-outs, hand-written drafts, running marginal notes, typewritten drafts, paste-ups—all these enter in various ways the idiosyncrasies of writers I know. While in the long run the use of such methods may remain idiosyncratic, I believe there is something to be learnt from a study of them as to the nature of intellectual processes.

The Timing of Writing

When accurate observation and analysis of the timing of speech have proved such a rewarding study, notably in the work of Dr. Goldman-Eisler, it is very surprising that so little has been done in this way with regard to writing. The only direct study we have found dates back to 1946.[8]

Anyone who has invigilated an examination will know how various are the patterns of pen-chewing behaviour. What do these pauses represent in the way of mental processes? Are they systematically related either to individuals or to kinds of writing assignment? How are they reflected in the quality and structures of the writing? How are they related—and here the examination room would be no place to investigate them—to strategies of drafting, revision and scanning ahead?

The 1946 study, 'Factors affecting regularity of the flow of words during written composition' by Van Bruggen, has no very enlightening answers to these questions, detailed though the investigation was. At age around 13 years, the investigator found, the best writers write in 'thought units', with a fairly rapid flow of words; a slow flow of ideas tends to be associated with a slow writing rate; familiarity with the material being handled increases the rate of flow; and pupils of *very low* and *very high* intelligence seem to have the fastest flow of words in writing. Unfortunately, the method of recording did not permit the investigator to study re-drafting beyond the simple crossing out and immediate rewriting of words or groups of words; if other kinds of emendation were made during the trials there is no mention of them. Looking back and looking forward, as indicated by retrospective revision, marginal notes and perhaps other devices, are likely to be of major significance in any study of how a writer uses the premeditation that writing permits.

In the Writing Research Unit, in 1967, we did in fact work out a procedure intended to produce a time-record matched word for word with the process of writing and revising a script throughout a single writing occasion, and analysing differences between individuals, differences between tasks by the same individual, and differences in the course of a single assignment. A senior colleague in the Department of Electrical Engineering at University College studied our requirements and was prepared to produce a prototype electronic transmitting pen to meet them. (This would have cost about £300 and would have required the purchase of a high-speed pen-recorder unit costing roughly the same again.) Neither time nor money was available then and the work remains to be done.

Kinds of Writing

The ubiquity of freshman composition courses in U.S. colleges has led to a great deal more American research in the field than has been done here. Yet no very powerful theoretical issues seem to emerge from it all. A glance through the NCTE publication *Research in Written Composition*[9] (1963), compiled after a two-and-a-half-year investigation by a small team, reveals a great many practical recommendations—some useful, some cancelling each other out—but does little to suggest the emergence of a framework which might give some coherence to the diverse enquiries. In indicating 'Unexplored Territory' the editors ask a number of questions such as, 'What are the effects of various kinds and amounts of reading on the quality and kinds of writing a person does?' Many of these questions make similar incidental references to 'kinds of writing', but the direct question, 'How may kinds of writing be described?' does not appear.

I attended in Minneapolis this November a three-day Seminar called by NCTE to consider 'Research design in English Education'. At the end of the period, the working party on Curriculum reported that their most urgent need was for 'more conceptual research, based on present knowledge and leading to new theoretical frameworks. . . . We need theoretical models which generate important research questions.' The working party on 'Composing and Speech' similarly reported its need for 'a theory of communicative competence'; that on Reading admitted that 'reading research is at present fragmented and at a preparadigmatic stage', and that on Language Development called what they were interested in 'discourse competence' and added that 'The discourse theory (still in reality a taxonomy) we have selected as the truest available is that developed by the London Writing Research Unit'.[10]

As far as writing is concerned, there can be no doubt that the need is above all to develop a theoretical framework, and that for lack of adequate descriptive categories much of the research being done in an educational context fails to generate theoretical insights and is even misleading in practice. Its view of writing as a process remains 'global'.

To quote one example: Kellogg Hunt[11] reported that his index of maturity in writing (the length of what he called a 'minimal terminable unit or T-Unit') showed significant differences in writing ability between writers of average IQ in grades 4, 8 and 12; but produced very curious results when applied to the work of adult novelists (Hemingway and Faulkner). Harold Rosen, as part of his doctoral thesis arising out of the work of the Writing Research Unit, applied the analysis to writings within function categories, and found a difference between poetic and transactional writing by 16-year-olds greater than Hunt's difference between grades 8 and 12. Moreover there was evidence to suggest that the more able writers were those who showed the greatest 'T-Unit' differences between one kind of writing and another.[12]

What the Writing Research team has done is merely a beginning, and this is not the place to go into that in any detail. We have devised two sets of categories, each set representing in the first instance a way of classifying writings produced in the secondary school. Ten categories cover the writer's 'sense of audience', ranging from 'self as audience' to 'a writer to his readers', and including four categories that represent rôles a teacher may take up (from 'child to trusted adult' to 'pupil to examiner'). The second set is of greater general interest and presents a framework I need for my further purposes here. It is a set of function categories based in part on a distinction first suggested in 1937 by D. W. Harding[13]—the distinction between using language in the rôle of participant and that of spectator. (Accepting the general view that man acts in the world of reality by means of, or in the light of, his *representation*, cumulatively built, of the world as he has experienced it, we may then observe that this leaves open to him an alternative mode of action—that of operating *directly upon his representation* without seeking an outcome in terms of the actual. It is activity of this latter kind that constitutes activity in the spectator rôle.)

Our scheme has three main categories:

(Participant rôle.................... Spectator rôle)
Transactional_____Expressive_____Poetic

'Expressive', the central term in the model, is taken from Sapir, who pointed out that all ordinary speech is mainly expressive, only to a limited degree referential. The governing convention might be interpreted as above all an assumption that the reader is interested in the writer and not merely in what he has to say about the world. Its function, centrally, is to explore 'togetherness' or exploit it. Developmentally, the expressive is a kind of matrix from which differentiated forms of writing will be evolved.

The more fully an utterance meets the demands of some kind of participation in the world's affairs, the nearer will it approach the transactional end of the scale: the more fully it satisfies spectator-rôle demands, the nearer it will move to the poetic end. The two movements are very different. Let us take 'informing' as an example of a function within the transactional; as expressive writing changes to meet the demands of this task it will become more explicit: that is, it will supply more of the context and will reflect a greater concern for accurate and specific *reference*; it will seek the kind of organisation that most effectively carries out such a task, and will exclude the personal, self-revealing features that might interfere with it.

To satisfy the demands of the spectator rôle, on the other hand, an utterance must become 'a verbal object'. Linguistic forms and the forms of whatever the language portrays will become the direct object of attention. What is afoot is evaluation, so that the feelings, attitudes, beliefs of the writer are paramount, and what is included in the utterance may be highly personal. It will be made intelligible to an audience of strangers by the complex and subtle internal structure of the artefact; private experience, that is to say, is given 'resonance' within the structure. A poetic utterance may be said to be a particular kind of self-presentation: not as an embodiment of local or transient or particular feelings but as a glimpse into the lifetime of feeling of the writer.[14]

Clearly the transactional category needs to be broken down in accordance with the kind of transaction undertaken; I shall not go into details here, but include an outline as appendix on p. 127.[15]

I have finally to suggest an important aspect of contrast between the two ends of the scale. Transactional utterances are contextualised in piecemeal fashion. We take what fragments interest us (from such an utterance as this paper, for example), reject the rest, build new connexions for ourselves between and around the fragments. But the poetic writer must resist such piecemeal contextualisation by his reader. His verbal object is a thing deliberately isolated from the rest of reality: to respond appropriately the reader must contextualise only *after* he has reconstructed the object in accordance with the complexity of its internal organisation. This we have called, 'global contextualisation', and the idea provides us with sub-categories of the poetic. Novelists do, for example, put over 'a message', and that message may be classified in accordance with the kind of transaction it involves: but to operate the conventions of the poetic, a message must be communicated in and through the verbal construct, the artefact *as a whole*. Thus, we would classify a novel such as Orwell's *Nineteen Eighty-Four* as 'poetic (persuasive)'.[16]

The De-contextualisation of Experience

These two modes of contextualisation provide me now with a fresh starting point. I wish to relate them to complementary processes of de-contextualisation on the part of the writer. I am very aware of my inability to take the enquiry far, but I can at least suggest the importance of the problems posed for our understanding of the rôle of writing in the processes of intellect.

Taking the view put forward in one form by Habermas[17] and another by Searle[18] that competence embraces two sets of rules, one grammatical and the other 'rules of use', I would suggest that the expressive function marks out an area of comparative freedom from the rules of use, and that as a writer moves from the expressive into the transactional he takes on responsibility for one set of rules of use, and responsibility for a different set as he moves from expressive into poetic. Further, that these two sets of rules of use constitute procedures for the de-contextualisation of human experience.

Psychologically speaking we are on familiar ground when we consider the de-contextualisation on the transactional side, because it must reflect the cognitive organisation that psychologists have studied for a century or more. Recently, speech acts analysis has begun to spell out the rules of discourse themselves. We have noted Harding's reference to the struggle to verbalise more and more of the non-verbal aspects of experience, and it is this achievement of speech that Habermas documents in describing the 'intersubjectively recognised rules' to which speech acts must conform. If private experience is to be brought into the public sphere in speech, there must be congruence between the parties at the level of word, action and gesture: there must be awareness on both sides of 'categorial differences between subject/object, outer/inner speech, private/public worlds'.[19]

There is a sense in which the writer—and I am thinking still of writing in the transactional function—in internalising his reader takes on a double responsibility, writer's and reader's, with regard to these rules. To illustrate at the very simplest level, it is in transactional writing that we encounter the difficulty of 'finding a way in' to a piece of writing. The intersubjectively recognised rules include, we have suggested, 'piecemeal contextualisation' by the reader: the writer thus seeks to enmesh with the reader's concerns at all points as he writes: and since context builds up step by step as the utterance proceeds,[20] the writer's difficulties are at their greatest as he begins to write. (Not for him Tolstoy's opening to *War and Peace*: '*Eh bien, mon prince*, so Genoa and Lucca are now no more than private estates of the Bonaparte family'; or Kingsley Amis' opening line to a poem, 'So, bored with dragons, he lay down to sleep.')

The struggle, the double responsibility, the ideal reader internalised—perhaps it is in these terms we can begin to justify our sense of the importance of writing in the field of cognitive activity.

It seems to me that work in speech acts analysis with regard to poetic utterance has done little more than indicate ways in which the rules set up for transactional discourse *do not* apply.[21] There is of course value in establishing a distinction by these means: but more positive definitions may not be forthcoming, I suspect, until we get on to another wave-length.

Towards this end, I shall turn to the pioneer work of Susanne Langer. From a reading, principally, of *Philosophical Sketches*[22] and *Mind: an Essay on Human Feeling*,[23] I would surmise that she believes we shall open a new chapter in psychology as we begin to understand the processes by which human experience is so organised as to produce a work of art. 'How little,' she says, 'any scientist can do with "contents of consciousness" the earnest efforts of great men have long demonstrated; how little can be done while ignoring the intraorganic climaxes of human mental acts psychologists great and small are still demonstrating. The fact is that people operating with familiar physicalist models do not see that the wraith-like character and mysterious coming and going of images and thoughts are a peculiarly interesting aspect of cerebral activity, which has never been studied or even precisely envisaged. The art symbol, however, reflects the nature of mind as a culmination of life, and what it directly exhibits, first of all, is the mysterious quality of intangible elements which arise from the growth and activity of the organism, yet do not seem entirely of its substance' (n. 23, op. cit., pp. 229–30).

Basic mental processes, elements of human consciousness (which she would characterise as feelings, in a broad sense) submit to two kinds of organisation: on the one hand one which results in cognitive structures, and on the other an organisation which results in works of art. I would add that, while the former requires a dissociation of cognitive from affective activity, the latter demands no such disjunction.

She is concerned, then, to lay bare the procedures by which an artist abstracts from experience, projects experience into an artistic construct. From Gestalt psychology she takes the idea of physiognomic perception and extends it to cover metaphorical transformations; from Freud, the concept of 'symbol' as he used it in accounting for dreams: 'Surely they are not established by any convention, and although they are related to quite other ideas, which they are said to "mean", they are not in any usual sense employed to refer to those ideas. They do not denote them for the dreamer as words denote their objects' (n. 22, op. cit., p. 61). And her own characteristic contribution is to suggest that the projection of tensions and resolutions 'which by their very occurrence . . . immediately generate structure' (n. 23, op. cit., p. 158) relates the work of art to living acts in a way not possible by discursive (transactional) means. But I can do no more than suggest—and succumb to—her analysis.

Alongside this essential and pioneer work, we need to pursue the observation and analysis, not of works of art only but of art-like activities at a lower level of intensity. It seems likely that the principles of organisation to be derived—the new chapter in psychology—may be used to describe a great deal of everyday human behaviour. Benveniste[24] has already suggested that style in language may best be accounted for in terms of Freud's dream symbols, a kind of unconscious ideation, and in the course of doing so presents interesting parallels to Langer's speculations about art. George Kelly[25] provides us with a general psychological framework based on the notion that is central to our model of language, and central to Langer's philosophy—that of man as *animal symbolicum*, to use Cassirer's terse formulation.

We need approaches at all levels, from the speculations of Susanne Langer to the specifications of speech acts analysis, if we are to understand the de-contextualisation procedures applicable to language in the spectator rôle, language along the functional spectrum from expressive to poetic.

Linguistic Exponents of the Taxonomy

If our sets of categories prove of value to research or teaching, as they show some signs of doing, it will be essential that our original design should be completed by enquiring what linguistic features, if any, prove to be their exponents. (I am prepared, in admitting that we have not done so, to blush with shame as often as is necessary.) This will involve taking scripts allotted to categories by our means—that is to say by the pooling of subjective judgements—and submitting them to linguistic analysis in search of partial correlates. Had we attempted to do this at an earlier stage, we should of course have short-circuited the experiment.

Some Pedagogical Problems Implied

Perhaps it is here for the first time that I directly tackle my brief. However, I make no apology for believing that we shall have little useful to say about how children learn to write, and hence about teacher behaviour, until we have a firmer conceptual grasp of what the activity means in linguistic, psychological and sociological terms. Meanwhile:

1. A major hypothesis in our four-year follow-up study is to the effect that most children, learning to write in school, will proceed by *dissociation*, by a differentiation of performance, successively, in face of differing demands. A great deal more evidence than we can supply will be needed to test the hypothesis adequately and investigate its ramifications.

2. To take one of these: if expressive writing facilitates a writer's access to the language resources recruited mainly through speech, part of the differentiation process will be by internalising written models. It is consistent with the general notion of dissociation to suppose that there will be a kind of shuttling between speech resources and the internalised written forms, and that this will have its own dynamic and take its own time. We need evidence to compare the effectiveness of deliberate writing to a model and the internalisation that accompanies reading for its own sake.

(There is always, of course, an alternative hypothesis to ours: that if you limp about long enough in somebody else's language you will learn to walk in it.)

3. We have observed that when children learn to write young, before going to school, they do not seem to conform to our hypothesis. For them the written language seems to exist (we suppose) for the purpose of producing books to be read to out of. Their early efforts in writing are usually contributions, make-believe or readable, to the world's stock of story-books. Should this motive be exploited with children in school, or would it prove a blind alley?

4. Our findings show, within transactional writing, a pattern of movement from lower levels of abstraction to higher, a pattern related to age and to curriculum subject. What kinds of intervention might assist this movement? A study of 'language across the curriculum' and the rôle of writing in learning throws up a multitude of problems of this nature.

5. We need to know a great deal more about the rôles a writer may take up, in relation to audience and function and

other variables, and the strategies with which he fulfils those rôles.

6. (a) It may be that a fuller understanding of the expressive function would reinforce the educational view that the speech of the home has a lifetime purpose to fulfil for any individual.

(b) Wherever an expressive form of speech exists, in any language or dialect, it is reasonable to suppose that this expressive speech is capable of being adapted to fulfil a poetic function.

(c) Social demands apart then (and these may be few), an individual's need of a widely acceptable form of language such as Standard English may be *essential* only in the case of written language in the transactional function. Such language, presumably, will continue to be required as long as the interchangeability of practical and intellectual knowledge is socially valued.

What are the implications of all this for the education of cultural minorities?

7. There is an urgent need for basic research and conceptual enquiry which will enable us to articulate with greater conviction our belief in the educational importance of the verbal arts and uses of language that are 'art-like'.

NOTES

1. Beckett, Samuel, *Malone Dies*, Penguin ed., Harmondsworth 1962, p. 25.
2. Harding, D. W., *Experience into Words*, Chatto & Windus, London 1963, p. 172.
3. Cassirer, Henry R., 'Visual communication and education', a paper read to the International Congress on Graphic Design and Education, Vienna 1971.
4. See McKellar, P., *Imagination and Thinking*, Cohen & West, London 1957, pp. 124–7.
5. Unpublished report by the London Association for the Teaching of English.
6. Moffett, James, *Teaching the Universe of Discourse*, Houghton Mifflin Co., Boston, Mass. 1968.
7. Wason, Peter, 'On writing scientific papers', *Physics Bulletin*, **21**, 1970, pp. 407–8.
8. Van Bruggen, John A., 'Factors affecting regularity of the flow of words during written composition', *Journal of Experimental Education*, **15** (2), December 1946. (Dr. Harold Rosen in fact discovered this in America while his colleagues in the Writing Research Unit were composing invisible letters to him.)

9. Braddock, R., Lloyd Jones, R., and Schoer, L., *Research in Written Composition*, National Council of Teachers of English, Champaign, Illinois 1963.

10. Unpublished Report, NCTE publication in the press.

11. Hunt, Kellogg, *Grammatical Structures Written at Three Grade Levels*, Research Report No. 3, NCTE, Champaign, Illinois 1965.

12. Rosen, Harold, unpublished Ph.D. thesis, University of London, 1968.

13. Harding, D. W., 'The rôle of the onlooker', *Scrutiny*, **VI** (3), 1937.

14. The idea is developed by Susanne Langer. See below, n. 23 (op. cit., p. 112).

15. For a brief account see my article, 'What's the use', in the *Educational Review* (Birmingham), **23** (3), *The Context of Language*, June 1971; reprinted in *Language in Education*, Open University and Routledge & Kegan Paul, London 1972.

    In reporting the work of the Writing Research Unit, I acknowledge the work of my colleagues Miss Nancy Martin, Dr. Harold Rosen, Messrs. Tony Burgess, Dennis Griffiths, Alex McLeod and Bernard Newsome.

16. This paragraph and the three that precede it are taken over with minor changes from an account to be published in the Proceedings of the UNESCO Seminar on the Teaching of English, Sydney, 1972.

17. Habermas, Jurgen, 'Systematically distorted communication' and 'Towards a theory of communicative competence', *Inquiry*, Nos. 3 and 4, 1971.

18. Searle, John, 'Chomsky's revolution in linguistics', Special Supplement, *The New York Review*, June 1972.

19. Habermas, first article referred to in n. 17, above.

20. See Lyons, John, *Structural Semantics*, Blackwell, Oxford 1963, pp. 83–4.

21. See Steinmann, Martin, Jr., 'Poems as Artifacts', paper presented at the Seventh International Congress for Aesthetics, Bucharest, 1972.

22. Langer, Susanne, *Philosophical Sketches*, Mentor Books, New York 1964.

23. Langer, Susanne, *Mind: An Essay on Human Feeling*, Vol. I, Johns Hopkins Press, Baltimore 1967.

24. Benveniste, Emile, *Problems in General Linguistics* (trans.), University of Miami Press, 1971, p. 74.

25. Kelly, George, *A Theory of Personality*, Norton, 1963.

Appendix

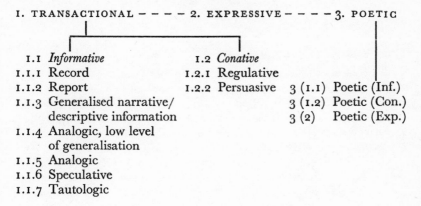

I. TRANSACTIONAL – – – – 2. EXPRESSIVE – – – –3. POETIC

1.1 *Informative*	1.2 *Conative*	
1.1.1 Record	1.2.1 Regulative	
1.1.2 Report	1.2.2 Persuasive	3 (1.1) Poetic (Inf.)
1.1.3 Generalised narrative/		3 (1.2) Poetic (Con.)
descriptive information		3 (2) Poetic (Exp.)
1.1.4 Analogic, low level		
of generalisation		
1.1.5 Analogic		
1.1.6 Speculative		
1.1.7 Tautologic		

SPEAKER'S INTRODUCTION

In my paper I have mentioned our work in the Writing Research Unit. But I have not set out to summarise our work or that of the researchers in this field. One of the things we find difficult in much of our research in language is how to cope with the total ongoingness of everything. There is an image that Polanyi[1] uses when he suggests that his unit of analysis is like an item in the strategy of the two players in a game of chess, involved together in the same event but operating quite independently. The unit has meaning then in terms of two quite different organised contexts. I like that image and have tried to relate it to human interaction in terms of language. But of course this double ongoingness, this multiple strategy on the part of each of the participants in any conversation, in any interaction, this seems to be the difficulty of our research.

It may be that when we look at writing we have here one way in which we may perhaps slow up the processes of interaction; by studying the processes involved in writing we may be able to discover something about the nature of the mental aspects of interaction.

I am very much aware that much of what we have said during this Seminar has been with regard to those uses of language that we call transactional. I want to deal with the other kinds (see the Appendix above) of which we know so little. I want to see the other kinds, the expressive and the poetic, operating as alternative modes of organisation to the cognitive, the analytic in a great many of our everyday activities. I think this is important educationally.

NOTE

1. Polanyi, M., *Personal Knowledge: Towards a Post-critical Philosophy*, Harper Torchbooks, New York 1964.

Discussant: *W. A. Gatherer*

Writing seems to have been the least studied of our pedagogical preoccupations; in contrast to the enormous body of research on reading, there has been very little systematic investigation of writing as a process. The London Writing Research Unit with which Professor Britton is associated is, I think, unique, and its findings and guidance will be important contributions to educational thinking and methods.

Our educational system puts a high value on writing as a social instrument. It is by far the most common medium of educational assessment, and it is the most widely used vehicle for the formal transmission of ideas. And yet there is an odd dissociation of writing from what we might call the 'normal' linguistic activities of our society. The behaviour settings in which the ordinary person employs writing are few and infrequent: after they have left school the majority of people stop having to write; except for an occasional letter they do little more than scribble a few notes. The amount of writing done may be a more emphatic marker of social variation than any other. We need to know more about the social ecology of writing.

At the same time, enculturation must include the teaching of writing, for the need to write is still widespread and important. It is essential that we should know more about the nature of writing both as an activity and as an artefact if we are to improve our ways of teaching it. Professor Britton touches upon all three aspects of this subject—the writing process, the descriptive analysis of what is written, and the pedagogical implications of these studies.

It is his schematic account of writing as text which has earned the most marked attention, and his present paper can profitably be read in association with his earlier reports in his essay, 'What's the Use?' and his book, *Language and Learning*. The schema he offers is useful particularly as an analytical instrument, enabling teachers to compare one written product with another in accordance with a number of systematised categories. The commentaries in Professor Britton's *Language and Learning* and in other applications of the model demonstrate how actual specimens of children's writing can be discussed in terms of the categories. But it is one thing to employ such a model for illustrating the differentiating characteristics of given texts; it is quite another thing to suggest that the categories reflect children's habits of thought and developmental progress.

These categories are theoretical constructs, and it remains to be seen how productive they prove in empirical trials. Will the categories stand up to widespread application in the field? Or will they tend to be fragmented more and more into subdivisions and sub-subdivisions until they disintegrate and disappear? Bill Messer's article, 'A lesson for the teacher',[1] illustrates this tendency: in his analysis of the speech and writing of 11-year-olds he says, 'The movement from the expressive to the different levels of the transactional should be envisaged as a continuum with the speaker moving in and out of these quite freely.' This is admittedly said of speech; but if, as seems likely, the same can be said of children's writing in most situations, then the categories can be little more than aids toward the subjective description of styles. As such they are of course extremely valuable to the teacher.

It would be interesting to know how, if at all, these categories relate to other classifications of types of language or discourse. How, for example, do Britton's subdivisions of the transactional function relate to Joos's five styles of discourse? Do Britton's categories parallel, or reflect, or overlap with Halliday's seven uses of language?[2] Is Britton's *transactional* related to Halliday's *instrumental, regulatory*, and *interactional* models? Is Britton's *expressive* related to Halliday's *personal* function? Is Britton's *poetic* function related to Halliday's *imaginative* model? If there are more than merely terminological distinctions to be drawn between one set of categories and another we should know what they are.

Professor Britton refers to the process of writing. I agree that we need to know much more about the nature and effects of premeditation; but this is only one of the factors in the process which require investigation. We will not fully understand what writing is as an activity—and consequently how best to go about teaching the skills—until there is more knowledge available about the cognitive, psychological and psychophysical processes that make up the act. Professor Britton suggests, here and elsewhere, that there is a relationship between the *kinds of composition* defined by his schema and *ways of composing*. For instance, in his paper he says that 'developmentally, the expressive is a kind of matrix from which differentiated forms of writing will be evolved'; and in 'What's the use?' he refers to the 'clear developmental implications' of the schema. The suggestion, I take it, is that the expressive mode is the most natural, perhaps the most primitive, of the writing functions. It gives the child access to his prior linguistic resources in spoken intercourse. It resembles, one might suppose, egocentric or social speech, and in so far as it does it will be less subject to the rules which govern transactional writing.

There is no evidence to show any kind of psychological reality to these categories or to the process hypothesised here. Yet it is a persuasive and highly employable theory: as the child moves from mastery of the expressive to mastery of the transactional functions he is acquiring techniques for making his written utterances more explicit, more specifically referential. This requires 'rules' of a particular kind. The creation of a 'poetic' utterance requires mastery of another, not necessarily completely different, set of rules, or techniques, or skills. It would need large-scale analysis of written texts produced by children over a period of years to show whether or not there is a gradual mastering of different rules or techniques, whether or not there is a progression from the expressive to the transactional and poetic functions as the individual matures and becomes more skilful. It will be interesting to see what evidence there is in the published work of the Schools Council Project, *Writing Across the Curriculum*, which is so powerfully sustained by Professor Britton's ideas.

The theory does not appear to throw much light upon the process of beginning writing. The reductive pressures that bear upon the child learning to write (apart from the technical handicaps, the lack of manual dexterity, etc.) urgently require investigation: the relative sparsity of symbols at the child's disposal, his lack of familiarity with the tactic and spelling rules of written language, the absence in the writing situation of stimulus and feedback. The 'rules of use' or pragmatic universals which are inherent in a speech act, and which complement and support the linguistic features of a spoken utterance, are not available to the writer except in so far as he 'invents' or 'postulates' an 'internalised other'. Professor Britton suggests that in expressive writing there is less constraint from the rules of use; that it is in transactional writing that we encounter the task of having to 'enmesh with the reader's concerns', thus attempting to re-create imaginatively the conditions of a speech act. I believe he makes too little of the tasks of formalisation that any act of writing imposes on the child; if we knew more about these we might understand much more about writing as a form of communication and as a form of artistic expression. But his suggestion that mature writing in the transactional mode is partly a matter of internalising an ideal reader is, in my view, a very powerful one that could yield valuable insights into the cognitive, linguistic and situational components of the writing process.

NOTES

1. Messer, Bill, 'A lesson for the teacher', *English in Education*, **6**, No. 3, 1972; *From Information to Understanding*, Schools Council, London 1972.
2. Halliday, M. A. K., 'Relevant models of language', in *The State of Language*, University of Birmingham, 1969.

GENERAL DISCUSSION

T. Brown   I should like to make a point about the categories (Appendix, page 127). I am worried about the tremendous breadth that *expressive* seems to cover. I am also worried in that it is never very clear to me whether *expressive* refers to spoken transactions or to interactions of a written kind. There is a failure here, I suggest, to acknowledge the difference between the written and the spoken. Unless this is done teachers will be confused when they try to apply the categories them-selves to children's writing.

Jessie Reid Thinking in terms of functions it seems to me that the demand to learn to write is imposed on the child by the educational system; most of the writing done by the child at school is transactional where the child is showing the teacher what he can do and what he knows.

Halliday I have found in trying to relate different taxonomies of functions that they do not fit and that they always leave gaps. This is not surprising since a taxonomy will always be seen in terms of the purpose for which it is designed. But I want to make a plea for any scheme of functions to face both ways, both into the language and out of the language. This means that Britton should be prepared to say some-thing about the linguistic realisations of the categories he has set up. When we say, for example, that a particular text is predominantly transactional, but that it also has a poetic component, then we are saying, in effect, that the writer has drawn on certain areas from his total linguistic potential.

Britton I have to agree with Halliday that a much more vigorous look than we have given, an analytic look, at the clues on which we are relying in making our judgements is necessary. But it is a big job.

Margaret Clark I have been interested in the extent to which the structure of the writing lesson in school has actually prevented the child from producing something that satisfies him. Children can be en-couraged to be satisfied with progressively more complicated execution and learn to use strategies to develop more satisfactory written pro-duction. I wonder if there are enough of the types of strategy in the planning and execution of written performance that we, for example, have gone through in preparing our papers for this Seminar, drafting, re-drafting, built in to the school teaching interaction.

Davies May I ask two questions? The first relates to unhappy writing, unhappy in the sense of not successful. Did you find, for example, pieces of writing that were clearly trying to belong to certain of your categories but did not really belong? The second question is whether you could expect to have sufficient linguistic indications available when you do that part of the analysis to tell you why you took up certain clues in order to place the pieces of writing in the various categories.

Britton I did not, of course, come here to report on the work we have been doing. However, I shall try to answer those questions. In answer to the first, we have tried to set up categories that are not normative categories, in such a way that teachers can make use of them. But our emphasis has been a *developmental* one, working in schools, with teachers, in order to get new hypotheses, new texts in new ways in the situations concerned. What we did notice immediately was that when writing tasks are assigned by somebody else, as is the normal case in schools, then one of two things is likely to happen: either you are going to make it your own or you are not. Then as to the function labels we gave our categories, we realised, of course, that they were adult-based. When we came to try to apply these to schools we found they had to be changed. There are special *school* categories, as well as pseudo-categories created by the teacher's demands.

As to the second question, we expect only partial corroboration of our categories in terms of linguistic markers, and these are intended for research purposes, not for teachers, who must continue to use their own subjective judgements.

Joan Tough   I would like to challenge your approach to the expressive function. It seems to me that the expressive process is as important to one's appraisal of the world as the analytic process. We do not capitalise in schools on the child's ability to project from his own inner world into somebody else's inner world. That is why the school learning process appears as a cognitive process, when it should be an expressive one too.

Britton   Tom Brown made a point related to yours. Some of the things children write down are written-down intimate speech, often more like jottings than sentences. This to us is expressive writing. We cannot say that this is not right—it has obviously found its way on to the page in this form.

Halliday   There is an important distinction that is worth making between formal and informal conversation as regards 'sentence' structure. The latter, i.e. informal conversation, as it goes on in houses, etc., is made up of sentences; it is highly structured and has few loose ends. Formal conversation such as in this Seminar, is quite the reverse.

Bernstein   It seems to me important to stress the expressive function. It is a function which has often been neglected and because it has been neglected, the psychological realities of children have not been made active in school. But I also think that there are various ways in which the imagination of man can work on the world. The expressive one is critical; it is not the only one, of course, but in your diagram (page 127) I think you have perhaps too much in the transactional category and too little in the expressive one.

Britton We have not today tackled the distinction which would enable us to define the poetic function. This is really central to what we are after. I agree that the imagination does work in various ways—you can be imaginative about fairies just as well as about ball-bearings. But still the analytic is an important part of life and it is so important because it gets the 'me' out of things, enforces a self-denying ordinance. We pay a price for this necessary human achievement in terms of fragmentation. But the division into modes like analytic and expressive is the analyst's division. To the child there is no split since what we feel and think about situations are all part and parcel of those situations.

Other points were made in the discussion by:
J. Sinclair
A. Sloman
H. Nathan

6

Chairman's Remarks and Summary

BASIL BERNSTEIN

I want to give my own impressions: they are in no way intended to serve as a summary of what has been said. Three points strike me as important:

1. The topics could have been reversed; several people have suggested this, and it might have been a way of relating the more theoretical topics that in fact came first more closely to the rather specific practical problems raised by Clark and Britton.

2. Linguistics has been mentioned several times, but nobody has raised the question as to what is available in linguistics for the description of various types of speech acts. Often linguistic theory determines what acts of speech are analysed rather than the acts themselves determining the theory. So I would call attention to the need for fundamental theoretical work in linguistics. For example Halliday has been developing theories which are particularly illuminating with regard to some of the problems I have been interested in, problems concerned with the social processes underlying the use of language in cultural transmission. Sinclair's work in the area of discourse is important if we are to understand the sequencing rules used by speakers in different contexts. There are too many different kinds of linguistics today to talk, as we have done, of 'linguistics'. Too often, also, theories which have a high degree of formality will shape the problem that we are interested in before being submitted to empirical investigation themselves. So I raise this issue of the need for fundamental work in linguistics.

3. When we talk about language and learning, or language in relation to learning, it seems to me that we are considering transmission and acquisition. Now the tragedy is that the study of acquisition and the study of transmission have gone on independently. Transmission–acquisition should be seen as a single matrix. We can see from the discussion that the two have been considered separately; for example Halliday is much more concerned with transmission and Bruner with acquisition. The result is a *strong* classification of unrelated theoretical systems so that the behaviour we are trying to understand is fragmented by the forms of thought we take to understand it. We have to bring the two together and then ask ourselves: what is the rôle of

language in the transmission–acquisition matrix? Language is given this central importance and then we can ask all kinds of questions. This matrix can be seen as the local social structure and we can ask questions about the relationship between a transmission–acquisition (TA) matrix in the home and a TA matrix in the school, and under what conditions is there conflict. So I would re-formulate the whole problem in terms of a TA matrix.

GENERAL DISCUSSION

Halliday I want to comment on what has been said about linguistics. It is true that there has been a shift in perspective. During the 1960s the predominant school rejected anything to do with context; a striking illustration of this occurs in John Lyons' seminal text *Introduction to Theoretical Linguistics*[1] where he says something to the effect that linguistics is not concerned with language in situation. I hope we are getting a better perspective now, supplementing that view with one that takes the context into account. There is a great deal of work going on in context-based studies, with a spate of recent publications with some such title as 'A theory of text'. Now although they are all getting bogged down in the attempt to be descriptive and explanatory (in terms of the nature of the linguistic system) at the same time, it seems to me that this attempt to link description and explanation is quite properly the goal of current linguistic theory and this goal will only be achieved by a whole lot of different kinds of study. Now may I come back to an earlier point (page 26). I would like to see this Seminar having two different kinds of result, first an emphasis on the need for research—fundamental linguistic research such as Bernstein has suggested—second, an emphasis on what I have called 'exploration' in which teachers and students work together creatively and excitingly to lead one another to a genuine furthering of understanding of language. And I hope we may be able this afternoon to identify suitable areas for such exploration.

Gatherer I like 'exploration'. Up to now I have used the term 'action research' but in future I propose to call it 'exploration'. This seems to me the truly modern way of in-service training for teachers. But I do have one doubt in my mind. Teachers are both busy and sceptical about the value to them of research. They are willing to help if they can be shown how. So I think we have to specify quite clearly what the topics are that would lend themselves to fruitful 'exploration'.

Davies I wonder whether it really *is* the job of teachers to take part in research. And what exactly is it that they are supposed to be doing better that they are not doing at the moment? We heard yesterday that in terms of dialect by the age of ten most children seem to cope. Could we say the same kind of thing about reading? Could it be that, as Bernstein suggested, we are forcing our description to fit categories and making things into problems that are not really so?

Sloman We have had experience of a real problem with our 5-year-old son, a problem of the sort Merritt discussed this morning. He had worked out for himself some highly individual reading strategy which worked. He was making very rapid progress and loving it, and then his teacher suddenly started asking him to name indicated letters on cards. He didn't understand what his teacher was trying to do, which was, in any case, refuted on every page of his reading book because the letter 'o' has various sounds. Anyway, the result now is that he will not read, does not like reading, has developed a reading neurosis.

Marie Clay Teachers must forget the idea that there is one best way of learning to read. There are many ways, many strategies, and teachers need to observe children to see what strategies they are using.

Widdowson Following up the notion about the use of linguistics for the language teacher, it seems to me that being made aware of how linguistics operates can be very useful for the language teacher. Of course, the whole problem of discourse is very much in the air at the moment, and it is a good thing to see that linguists are at last turning their attention to it. Now there are, I think, three features of written discourse that can be meaningful to the language teacher. All of them have been mentioned directly or indirectly in this Seminar. First, written discourse is non-reciprocal; the transfer from the use of spoken to the use of written discourse is a change in the mode of communication from reciprocal to non-reciprocal. This has implications for oral reading, since oral reading involves, as it were, making non-reciprocal communication, thus relating it to what the child already has. Second, written discourse is very little used, as Gatherer reminded us. So we may be trying to teach children something that adults do not do, cannot do, something highly artificial. Third, written discourse is, after all, an extension of what has already been learned in terms of structure in another mode.

Halliday I agree that written discourse has been neglected, but I do not see any need for choice here. Both text and discourse can be and need to be studied.

Joan Tough There are necessarily different kinds of research. There is the research worker's kind, developing the theory and providing the tools. Then there is the research that has to do with how you teach.

The one enables the other to go on, but the teacher cannot always wait for the linguist to give him the necessary tools. So the teacher has to get on with his own research as best he can. I myself think that something of the sort mentioned by Clark would be very suitable to try out in classrooms, i.e. looking at the strategies employed by successful mothers and then adapting them for classroom use. By intensifying what these successful mothers are doing we may be able to enlarge the range of uses that their strategies have.

Jessie Reid   The suggestion has been made that observation is not the teacher's job. May I say that I very much disagree with this. Observation is an essential part of the teacher's job, since it makes them more aware of language and more able to relate the ongoing elements in the classroom discourse to an overall classification and respond to those elements.

Speitel   I should like to see language 'exploration' for fun not only to solve problems for the teacher. Even if dialect ceases to be a problem by the age of 10 it can still provide this kind of exploration. But of course it does not cease to be a problem in Scotland—in Aberdeenshire for example.

Sinclair   I should like to probe into the relation between language and all other kinds of learning since in the last thirty years or so it seems as though we have taken language as the great analogy for human learning. But I am not sure that it should always be an analogy.

Merritt   In spite of what Halliday said I think there are priorities, certainly in the teaching of reading, where, it seems to me, research must start at the top. By the top I mean reading purposes. Reading is a tool which we use to acquire information and what we need to know is just what kinds of information. So the starting point with reading must not be at the skill level—it must be a question of the variety of printed media which people are going to have to cope with in their school lives and thereafter. Until there has been an exhaustive survey of the kinds of printed media which provide the information people require, the teaching of reading has not even started.

Bernstein   That would involve a vast demographic survey with the creation of incredibly complex taxonomies.

Bruner   I need to express a puzzlement here. It seems to me that two possibly complementary modes of approach to language are constantly being discussed. In the first, in linguistics proper, as it were, we look at language opaquely, to see the structure. In the second, the transparent way, we look at language to see what it is used for. And of course there are many sad accounts of teachers converting in their teaching from the second to the first so that children are suddenly asked to study a verb conjugation and vow they will never go to another Latin class. Clearly in language learning we simply cannot use the formal approach of the structural linguist. So what needs to be done, I suggest, is to look at kinds of situation of use in which there are the maximum opportunities for learning the structures that are to be converted for use. Let me give some examples:

1. Writing—there is no naturalistic account of what people use writing for. I would bet my bottom dollar that most of the writing people do is of the 'Don't leave milk today' kind of message to the milkman. Either simple commands of this kind or sequence instructions like 'Turn left to get to George Street and then turn right.'

2. Tutor theory—I was delighted to hear Clark tell us about her study of 'successful' mothers of early readers. I recently tried to find something on the theory of the tutor—when there is any assisted instruction at all. There are lots of theories about it but I could not find a single paper that dealt in detail with the different kinds of assistance given by adults to children. I am afraid that whoever is going to finance this kind of work has to accept that it will be very low-level research. But very necessary.

3. Language and culture—Halliday made the point that the main thing we do with language is to transmit culture. I think that is only very partially true. I want to argue that one of the main things we are doing when we transmit is to attempt disambiguation. In other words the point of communication very often is to try to reach agreement on a common referent, on which people can join together. We know very little about techniques of disambiguation in other than face-to-face discourse.

4. Transmission and acquisition—what is really needed here, I think, is to get on with the task of studying the acquisition of transmission. Do not, that is, stop your study of Adam and Eve when they have mastered the acquisition. Go on as they now learn to acquire transmission. We are trying to do something of this kind, to build up a code that has in it something I should like to call 'vicarious functioning'. It tries to look at the different codes people work with that may be substitutable for one another and asks the question whether there is not some way in which in effect we carry around different code books.

So to come back to Bernstein's initial point, how can Halliday talk only about transmission and Bruner only about acquisition? How indeed! I think it comes from the fact that we have gone far enough in our respective enterprises for each to know that he cannot deal with the nature of the transmission or the acquisition aspect until he finds out more about the nature of the formal code. And I certainly cannot move on to the question of how the code is learned unless I put things into a much more sociolinguistic context, in which I find out why they are transmitting, to what end, and what permits correction between people.

Merritt Can I comment on the parent-child relationship in reading because I think I have been misunderstood here. What I tried to say was that parents should not *teach* children to read. What they should do is to provide the opportunities for learning—and I referred to a whole set of intrinsics that could be used. I also said that older children can be taught how to help younger ones, in a kind of 'parent' rôle, thus bringing about the greater understanding so conducive to learning which we have been talking about.

Davies I should like to make a point about the language varieties question. It has come up several times and it has been criticised by our Chairman because of the taxonomic multiplication that follows. One of the things that struck me, in looking at the kinds of material that children, in the upper primary and lower secondary school, are given to read, is not how different they are but how much they are the same. Now they are supposed to be different—if one takes the operational approach of saying that reading in different school subjects is different. But if my guess is right and they are in fact very much the same, does this not suggest that children are not being given sufficient variety of experience in reading? This, of course, would have an effect on the kinds of understanding children have of other cultures, other ways of approaching politics, etc.

Halliday I agree with this. The reason is, I suggest, that adults' model of language functions is too simplistic. We *think* one text is different from another because one happens to be talking about football and another about radio or something. In fact they may be very much the same. I like Merritt's notion. I think some kind of survey could be of help, in the way Davies has suggested, giving us a valuable perspective on the sort of language experience that children in school can be helped to at different ages. Of course I know there would be problems and taxonomic multiplication. I still think it would be useful.

T. Brown I want to take up Bruner's point about writing. It may be that it ceases to be of social use to most school children. But the fact is, I suggest, that we could not carry on the process of education without writing. I think it would be useful to know just what is the rôle of writing in the primary school. Moreover, I should like to suggest that the more you write, the better perhaps you read. Again, it may be that the more differently you can write, the more you can cope with this problem of varieties of language, the more you imbibe in school something that you need to have as an adult.

Bernstein   I feel that we need to widen the terms of our discussion in order to get any understanding of learning if indeed learning is seen in terms of my TA matrix. We need to ask the basic question of how the distribution of power and the principles of control affect this TA matrix. I would want to look at language in use in terms of the rules which create order in the matrix (control) and in terms of the maintenance and repetition of the matrix (power). This would give me a dynamic framework.

Bruner   Doesn't that—if not politicise—at least sociologise the topic? Power and control, yes, but that leaves out a great deal, all the intra-personal uses of language.

Halliday   I should like to correct a misquotation. Bruner said I used the phrase 'language is mainly used in cultural transmission'. I could not write something like that.

Other points were raised in the discussion by:
   P. Griffiths
   J. Britton
   Elisabeth Ingram
   Margaret Clark
   H. Nathan
   Mrs. N. Francis

NOTE

1. Lyons, John, *Introduction to Theoretical Linguistics*, C.U.P., Cambridge 1968.

Bibliography

Abramyan, L. A., 'Organization of the voluntary activity of the child with the help of verbal instruction.' Unpublished diploma thesis, Moscow University, 1958. Cited by A. R. Luria, *The Role of Speech in the Regulation of Normal and Abnormal Behavior*, Liveright, New York 1961.

Ammon, U., 'Dialekt als sprachliche Barriere. Eine Pilotstudie über Schwierigkeiten von Dialektsprechern im Schulaufsatz', in *Muttersprache*, **82** (1972), pp. 224–237.

Anthony, A., *et al.*, *Edinburgh Articulation Test, Textbook*, Edinburgh 1971.

Austin, J. L., *How to do Things with Words: The William James Lectures delivered at Harvard University in 1955*, ed. J. O. Urmson, Clarendon Press, Oxford 1962.

Bar-Hillel, Y., *Language and Information*, Addison-Wesley, Reading, Mass.; and Jerusalem Academic Press, Jerusalem 1964.

Bartlett, F. C., *Remembering: a Study in Experimental and Social Psychology*, Cambridge University Press, Cambridge 1932.

Becket, Samuel, *Malone Dies*, Penguin ed., Harmondsworth 1962.

Benveniste, Emile, *Problems in General Linguistics* (trans.), University of Miami Press 1971.

Bernstein, B., 'Social class and linguistic development: A theory of social learning,' in *Education, Economy and Society*, A. H. Halsey, J. Floud, and C. A. Anderson (eds.), Free Press, Glencoe, Illinois 1961.

— 'A sociolinguistic approach to socialization: with some references to educability', in *Language and Poverty*, Markham Press, F. Williams (ed.), Chicago 1970.

— *Class, Codes and Control. Vol. I: Theoretical Studies Towards a Sociology of Language*, Routledge & Kegan Paul (Primary Socialization, Language & Education), London 1971.

Blank, M. 'Some philosophical influences underlying pre-school intervention for disadvantaged children', F. Williams (ed.), in *Language and Poverty*, Markham Press, Chicago 1970, pp. 62–80.

Bloom, Lois, *Language Development: Form and Function in Emerging Grammars*, MIT Press, Cambridge, Mass. 1970.

Bowerman, Melissa, 'Learning to talk: A cross-linguistic study of early syntactic development with special reference to Finnish'. Unpublished doctoral dissertation, Harvard University, 1970.

Braddock, R., Lloyd Jones, R., and Schoer, L., *Research in Written Composition*, National Council of Teachers of English, Illinois 1963.

Brandis, W., and Henderson, D., *Social Class, Language and Communication*, Routledge & Kegan Paul, London 1970.

Britton, J. M., *Language and Learning*, Allen Lane, The Penguin Press, Harmondsworth 1970.

— 'What's the Use', *Educational Review* (Birmingham), **23** (3), *The Context of Language*, June 1971; reprinted in *Language in Education*, Open University and Routledge & Kegan Paul, London 1972.

Broadbent, D. E., 'Role of auditory localization and attention in memory span', *J. Exp. Psychology*, **47,** 1954, pp. 191–6.

— *Perception and Communication*, Pergamon Press, London 1958.

Bruner, J. S., 'Poverty and childhood.' Presented on the occasion of the Annual Citation Award of the Merrill-Palmer Institute, Detroit, Michigan, 9 June 1970.

— 'The nature and uses of immaturity', *American Psychologist*, **27** (8); 1972, pp. 1–22.

— Goodnow, J., and Austin, G. *A Study in Thinking*, New York: Wiley, 1956.

— Olver, R. R., and Greenfield, P. M., *Studies in Cognitive Growth*, Wiley, New York 1966.

Campbell, R., and Wales, R., 'The study of language acquisition', J. Lyons (ed.), *New Horizons in Linguistics*, Penguin, Harmondsworth 1970.

Cassirer, Henry R., 'Visual communication and education'. A paper read to the International Congress on Graphic Design and Education, Vienna 1971.

Cazden, C. B., 'The neglected situation in child language research and education', in F. Williams (ed.), *Language and Poverty*, Markham Pub. Co., Chicago 1970.

— 'Three sociolinguistic views of the language of lower-class children—with special attention to the work of Basil Bernstein', *Developmental Medicine and Applied Neurology*, 1971.

— *Child Language and Education*, Holt, Rinehart & Winston, New York 1972.

Chomsky, C., *The Acquisition of Syntax in Children from 5 to 10*, Research Monograph No. 57, The MIT Press, Cambridge, Mass., 1969.

Chomsky, N., *Chomsky: Selected Readings*, ed. J. Allen and P. van Buren, Oxford University Press, London 1971.

— *Aspects of the Theory of Syntax*, MIT Press, Cambridge, Mass. 1965.

Clark, M. M., *Reading Difficulties in Schools*, Penguin Papers in Education, Penguin, Harmondsworth 1970.

Clay, M. M., *Reading: The Patterning of Complex Behaviour*, Heinemann Educational Books, Auckland 1972.

— *The Early Detection of Reading Difficulties—A Diagnostic Survey*, Heinemann Educational Books, Auckland 1972.

Cole, M., and Bruner, J. S., 'Cultural differences and inferences about psychological processes', *American Psychologist*, **26** (10), 1971, 867–76.

— Gay, J., Glick, J. A., Sharp, D. W., *et al.*, *The Cultural Context of Learning and Thinking: an Exploration In Experimental Anthropology*, Basic Books, New York 1971.

— and Scribner, S., 'The cognitive consequences of formal and informal education.' Paper presented at meeting of the American Association for the Advancement of Science, Washington, D.C. 1972.

Cook-Gumperz, Jenny, *Socialization and Social Control: a Study of Social Class Differences in the Language of Maternal Control*, Routledge & Kegan Paul (Primary Socialization, Language & Education), London 1973.

Dale, Philip S., *Language Development: Structure and Function*, Dryden, Hinsdale, Ill. 1972.

Davies, D., Julian, M., and Isard, Stephen, D. 'Utterances as programs.' Paper submitted to the 7th International Machine Intelligence Workshop, Edinburgh, June 1972.

De Laguna, G. A., *Speech: Its Function and Development*. Indiana University Press, Bloomington 1927.

Doughty, Peter, Pearce, John, and Thornton, Geoffrey, *Exploring Language*, Edward Arnold, London 1972.

Douglas, Mary, 'Do dogs laugh? a cross-cultural approach to body symbolism', *Journal of Psychosomatic Research*, **15**, p. 389.

Downing, J., 'How children think about reading', *The Reading Teacher*, **23**, iii, 1969, pp. 217–30.

— and Thackray, D. V., *Reading Readiness*, University of London Press Ltd., London 1971.

Duncker, K., 'On problem solving' (trans. by L. S. Lees), *Psychological Monographs*, **58**, 1945.

Fillmore, C. J., 'The case for Case', in E. Bach, and R. Harmes (eds.), *Universals in Linguistic Theory*, Holt, Rinehart & Winston, New York 1968.

Fry, D. B., 'Speech reception and perception', *New Horizons in Linguistics*, in J. Lyons (ed.), Penguin, Harmondsworth 1970, pp. 29–52.

Gahagan, D. M., and Gahagan, G. A., *Talk Reform: Exploration in Language for Infant School Children*, Routledge & Kegan Paul, London 1970.

Gardner, R. A., and Gardner, B. T., 'Teaching sign language to a chimpanzee', *Science*, **165**, 1969, 664–72.

Gatherer, W. A., 'Extending reading efficiencies', in M. M. Clark and A. Milne (eds.) *Reading and Related Skills*, Ward Lock Educational, London, in press.

Goffman, E., 'The neglected situation', in J. Gumperz and D. Hymes (eds.), *The Ethnology of Communication, American Anthropologist*, **66** (6, pt. 2), 1964, p. 133.

— *Relations in Public*, Allen Lane, The Penguin Press, Harmondsworth 1971.

Goldstein, K., *Human Nature in the Light of Psychopathology*, Harvard University Press, Cambridge, Mass. 1940.

— 'Concerning rigidity', *Character and Personality*, **11**, 1943, pp. 209–26.

Goodman, K. S., 'Reading: A psycholinguistic guessing game', in H. Singer and R. B. Ruddell (eds.), *Theoretical Models and Processes of Reading*, International Reading Association, Newark, Delaware, 1970.

Greenberg, J., *Universals of Language*, MIT Press, Cambridge, Mass. 1963.

Greenfield, P. M., 'Oral or written language: The consequences for cognitive development in Africa and the United States.' Paper presented at the Symposium on cross-cultural cognitive studies, American Educational Research Association, Chicago 1968.

— Smith, J. H., and Laufer, B., *Communication and the Beginnings of Language; the Development of Semantic Structure in One-word Speech and Beyond*, Academic Press, New York, in press.

Grice, H. P., 'Meaning', in P. F. Strawson (ed.), *Philosophical Logic*, Oxford University Press, London 1967.

Habermas, Jurgen, 'Introductory remarks to a theory of communicative competence', *Inquiry*, **13**, 3, 1970. Reprinted in H. P. Dreitsel (ed.), *Recent Sociology*, No. 2, Macmillan, London.

— 'Systematically distorted communication' and 'Towards a theory of communicative competence', *Inquiry*, Nos. 3 and 4, 1971.

Halliday, M. A. K., 'Relevant models of language', in *The State of Language*, University of Birmingham, 1969.

— *Explorations in the Functions of Language*, Edward Arnold (Explorations in Language Study), London 1973.

— *Language and Social Man*, Longman (Papers of the Programme in Linguistics and English Teaching, Second Series), London, in press.

— 'Learning how to mean', in E. and E. Lenneberg (eds.), *Foundations of Language Development: a Multidisciplinary Approach*, UNESCO & IBRO (International Brain Research Organization), in press.

— McIntosh, Angus, and Strevens, Peter, *The Linguistic Sciences and Language Teaching*, Longman (Longman's Linguistics Library), London 1964, Indiana University Press, Bloomington, Ind. 1966.

Harding, D. W., 'The role of the onlooker', *Scrutiny*, **VI** (3), 1937.

— *Experience into Words*, Chatto & Windus, London 1963.

Hardy, M. I. 'The development of beginning reading skills: Recent findings', M. M. Clark and A. Milne (eds.), *Reading and Related Skills*, Ward Lock Educational, London, in press.

Harman, D. 'A study of the structure of literacy campaigns'. D.Ed. thesis, Graduate School of Education, Harvard University 1972.

Hasan, Ruqaiya, *Language in the Imaginative Context: a Sociolinguistic Study of Stories Told by Children*, Routledge & Kegan Paul (Primary Socialization, Language & Education), London, in press.

Hasselberg, J. 'Die Abhängigkeit des Schulerfolgs vom Einfluss des Dialektes', in *Muttersprache*, **82** (1972), pp. 201–223.

Hunt, Kellogg, *Grammatical Structures Written at Three Grade Levels*, Research Report No. 3, NCTE, Illinois 1965.

Hymes, Dell H., 'Models of interaction of language and social setting', *J. Social Issues*, **23**, 1967.

— 'Linguistic theory and the functions of speech', *International Days of Sociolinguistics*, Rome 1969.

— 'Competence and performance in linguistic theory', in R. Huxley and E. Ingram (eds.), *Language Acquisition: Models and Methods*, Academic Press, London & New York 1971.

Inhelder, B., and Piaget, J. *Growth of Logical Thinking from Childhood to Adolescence*, Basic Books, New York 1958.

Jahoda, Marie and Thomas, Laurie, 'The Mechanics of Learning', *New Scientist*, 14 April 1966, pp. 114–17.

Jones, D., *Everyman's English Pronouncing Dictionary*, 12th ed., Dent, London 1963.

Kamii, C., 'Evaluation of learning in pre-school education: Socio-emotional, perceptual-motor, cognitive development', in B. S. Bloom, J. T. Hastings and G. F. Madaus (eds.), *Handbook on Formative and Summative Evaluation of Student Learning*, McGraw Hill, New York 1971, pp. 281–344.

Katz, J. J., and Fodor, J. A., 'The structure of a semantic theory', *Language*, **39**, 1963, pp. 170–210.

Keenan, E. L., 'Logic and language', *Daedalus*, **102** (3), 1973, pp. 183–94.

Keller, R. E., *German Dialects*, Manchester 1961, pp. 30ff.

Kelly, George, *A Theory of Personality*, Norton, 1963.

Krippner, S. 'The boy who read at eighteen months', *Exceptional Children*, **30**, 1963, pp. 105–9.

Labov, W., 'The logic of non-standard English', in F. Williams (ed.), *Language and Poverty*, Markham Press, Chicago 1970.

Langer, Susanne, *Philosophical Sketches*, Mentor Books, New York 1964.

— *Mind: An Essay on Human Feeling*, Vol. I, Johns Hopkins Press, Baltimore 1967.

Lashley, K. S., 'The problem of serial order in behaviour', in L. A. Jeffress (ed.), *Cerebral Mechanisms in Behaviour*, Wiley, New York 1951, pp. 112–36.

Liddell, 'Conditioning and Emotions', *Scientific American*, **190**, 1954, pp. 48–57.

Löffler, H., 'Mundart als Sprachbarriere', in *Wirkendes Wort*, **22** (1972), pp. 23–39.

Low, J. T., 'Scottish literature in the schools', *Scottish Literary News*, vol. 1, nos. 3 and 4, 1971.

Lyons, John, *Structural Semantics*, Blackwell, Oxford 1963, pp. 83–4.

— *Introduction to Theoretical Linguistics*, Cambridge University Press, Cambridge 1968.

Luria, A. R., *The Role of Speech in the Regulation of Normal and Abnormal Behaviour*, ed. J. Tizard, Pergamon Press, Oxford, 1961.

McCawley, J. D., 'The role of semantics in grammar,' in E. Bach and R. Harmes (eds.), *Universals in Linguistic Theory*, Holt, Rinehart & Winston, New York 1968, pp. 125–69.

Macauley, R. K. S., and Trevelyan G. D., *Language, Education and Employment in Glasgow*, A Report to the S.S.R.C. Vols. 1 & 2, 1973.

Mackay, D., Thompson, B., and Schaub, P., *Breakthrough to Literacy*, Teacher's Manual, Longman, London 1970.

McKellar, P., *Imagination and Thinking*, Cohen & West, London, pp. 124–7, 1957.

Macnamara, J., 'Cognitive basis of language learning in infants', *Psychological Review*, **79**, 1–13, 1972.

McNeill, D., 'The two-fold way for speech'. Paper presented at the CNRS Conference on Psycholinguistics, Paris, 1971.

Maier, N. R. F., 'Reasoning in humans, 1, On direction', *J. Comparative Psychology*, **10**, 1930, pp. 115–43.

Marshall, J. C., 'The biology of communication in man and animals,' in J. Lyons (ed.), *New Horizons in Linguistics*, Penguin, Harmondsworth 1970.

Martsignovskaya, E. N., 'Research into the reflective and regulatory role of the second signalling system of pre-school age'. Collected papers of the Department of Psychology, Moscow University, undated. Cited by A. R. Luria, *The Role of Speech in the Regulation of Normal and Abnormal Behavior*, Liveright, New York 1961.

Mead, G. H., *Mind, Self and Society: from the Standpoint of a Social Behaviorist*. University of Chicago Press, Chicago 1934.

Merritt, J. E., 'The intermediate skills: towards a better understanding of the process of fluent reading'. First published in K. W. Gardner (ed.), *Reading Skills: Theory and Practice*, Ward Lock Educational, London 1970. Subsequently published in J. M. Morris (ed.), *The First R: Yesterday, Today and Tomorrow*, Ward Lock Educational, London 1972.

— 'Reading failure: a re-examination,' in V. Southgate (ed.). *Literacy at All Levels*, Ward Lock Educational, London 1972, pp. 175–84.

Messer, Bill, 'A lesson for the teacher', *English in Education*, **6,** No. 3, 1972.
— *From Information to Understanding*, Schools Council, London 1972.
Miller, George A., *Toward a Third Metaphor for Psycholinguistics*, manuscript, 1973.
Moffett, James, *Teaching the Universe of Discourse*, Houghton Mifflin Co., Boston, Mass. 1968.
Moray, N. *Listening and Attention*. Penguin, Harmondsworth 1969.
Morris, C. W., *Signs, Language and Behavior*, Prentice-Hall, New York 1946.
— 'Foundations of the theory of signs', *Int. Encyc. of Unified Science*, 1, No. 2, Univ. of Chicago Press, Chicago 1938.
Morris, J. M., 'You can't teach what you don't know', in M. M. Clark and A. Milne (eds.), *Reading and Related Skills*, Ward Lock Educational, London, in press.
O'Connor, N., and Hermelin, B., *Speech and Thought in Severe Subnormality*, Pergamon Press, Oxford 1963.
Olver, R. R., and Hornsby, J. R., 'On equivalence', J. S. Bruner, R. R. Olver, P. M. Greenfield, *et al.*, in *Studies in Cognitive Growth*, Wiley, New York 1966.
Peirce, C. S., 'How to make our ideas clear', *Popular Science Monthly*, **12,** 1878, pp. 286–302.
Plato, *Meno*. trans. F. Sydenham, in *Five Dialogues*, ed. A. Lindsay, Dent, London 1910.
Polanyi, M., *Personal knowledge: Towards a Post-critical Philosophy*, Harper Torchbooks, New York 1964.
Pop, S., *La Dialectologie*, vol. 1. Louvain 1950.
Premack, D., 'Some general characteristics of a method for teaching language to organisms that do not ordinarily acquire it', in L. E. Jarrard (ed.), *Cognitive Processes of Non-human Primates*, Academic Press, New York 1971.
Reid, J. F., 'Learning to think about reading', *Educational Research*, **9,** 1966, pp. 56–62.
— 'Children's comprehension of syntactic features found in some extension readers,' in J. F. Reid (ed.), *Reading Problems and Practices*, Ward Lock Educational, London 1972, pp. 394–403.
Rosen, Harold, unpublished Ph.D. thesis, University of London, 1968.
Ryan, Joanna, 'Early language development', in M. P. M. Richards (ed.), *The Integration of the Child in the Social World*, in press.
Sacks, H., *Social Aspects of Language: the organisation of sequencing in conversation*, Prentice-Hall, Englewood Cliffs, N.J.
Sapir, E., *Language: An Introduction to the Study of Speech*, Harcourt, Brace and Co., New York 1921.
Schegloff, E. A., 'Sequencing in conversational openings', *American Anthropologist*, **70,** 1968, 1075–95.
Searle, J. R., *Speech Acts: an Essay in the Philosophy of Language*, Cambridge University Press, Cambridge 1969.
— 'Chomsky's revolution in linguistics', Special Supplement, *The New York Review*, June 1972.
Simon, H., *The Sciences of the Artificial*, MIT Press, Cambridge, Mass. 1969.
Slobin, D. I., 'Seven questions about language development', in P. C. Dodwell (ed.), *New Horizons in Psychology, II*, Penguin, Harmondsworth 1972.

Smith, F., *Understanding Reading*, Holt, Rinehart and Winston, New York 1971.

Smith, M. K., 'Measurement of the size of general English vocabulary through the elementary grades and high school', *Genetic Psychology Monographs*, **24**, 1941, pp. 311–45.

Smith, S., 'Language and non-verbal test performance of racial groups in Honolulu before and after a 14-year interval', *J. Gen. Psychology*, **26**, 1942, pp. 51–93.

Southgate, V., and Roberts, G. R., *Reading—Which Approach?* University of London Press, London 1970.

Speitel, H. H., *Some Studies in the Dialect of Midlothian*, Ph.D., Edinburgh 1969.

Start, K. B., and Wells, B. K., *The Trend of Reading Standards*, National Foundation for Educational Research in England and Wales, Slough 1972.

Sutherland, N. S., 'Visual discrimination of orientation and shape by the octopus', *Nature*, **179**, London 1957, pp. 11–13.

Templin, Mildred C., *Certain Language Skills in Children: Their Development and Interrelationships*, University of Minnesota Press, Minneapolis 1957.

— 'Relation of speech and language development to intelligence and socioeconomic status', *Volta Review*, **60**, 1958, pp. 331–4.

Tolman, E. C., *Purposive Behavior in Animals and Men*, The Century Co., New York 1932.

Treisman, A. M., 'Contextual cues in selective listening', *Q.J. Exp. Psychology*, **12**, No. 4, 1960, pp. 242–8.

Turner, Geoffrey J., 'Social class differences in the behaviour of mothers in regulative (social control) situations', University of London Institute of Education, Sociological Research Unit, forthcoming.

Ure, Jean, and Ellis Jeffrey, 'Register in descriptive linguistics and linguistic sociology', in Oscar Uribe Villegas (ed.), *Las concepciones y problemas actuales de la sociolingüística*, University of Mexico Press, Mexico City 1972.

Van Bruggen, John A., 'Factors affecting regularity of the flow of words during written composition', *J. Experimental Education*, **15** (2), December 1946.

Vygotsky, L. S., *Thought and Language*, ed. and trans. E. Hanfmann and G. Vakar, MIT Press, Cambridge, Mass., and Wiley, New York 1962.

Washburn, S. L., and Howell, F. C., 'Human evolution and culture', in S. Tax (ed.), *The Evolution of Man*, vol. 2, University of Chicago Press, Chicago 1960.

Wason, Peter, 'On writing scientific papers', *Physics Bulletin*, **21**, 1970, pp. 407–8.

Wepman, J. M., 'Auditory discrimination, speech and reading', *The Elementary School Journal*, **60**, 1960, pp. 325–33.

Wilkinson, A., *The Foundations of Language*, Oxford University Press, London 1971.

Abstract of Revised Paper by Bruner and Peterson

Language is considered as an instrument of thought, the one refining and developing the other. Analytic competence is introduced and distinguished from the two more widely discussed competences in language, linguistic competence and communicative competence. The possession of analytic competence enables different levels of abstraction to be established, for example it enables the child to go beyond the immediately obvious. Russian experiments are cited which suggest how language helps the child transcend the dominance of figure over ground. Analytic competence further requires the ability to shift attention from one feature to another and from whole to part. It is suggested that analytic competence is not evenly distributed among the population and is probably best acquired through formal education.

The exercise of performing analytic effective acts by the use of natural language is not so easy as testing for entailment and vacuity in formal language propositions. Four language aided heuristics are suggested as means of 'making our ideas clear'. These are: (a) transformations to increase explicitness (these involve the move to more highly formulated expressions of thought in order to use the grammatical properties of the language to elaborate the thought); (b) idealization (which may involve limit testing or arguing from the extreme case); (c) combinatorial expansion and restriction (which involves ordering the learners' mode of describing the array of instances); (d) explication of intent (which involves the speaker making clear first to himself and then to his listener what his intent is).

Bruner and Peterson argue, following de Laguna, that analytic competence is restricted to those occupied in intellectual pursuits. A community developing technically seems to create demands for more people with analytic competence and these are provided through formal education. What schools do is to decontextualize knowledge and to demand the use of analytic competence as a feature of the communicative competence of their members. Analytic competence is not difficult to achieve, given the right community to be nurtured in. Bruner and Peterson conclude that analytic competence is made possible by the possession of communicative competence; but a society must first express a need for analytic competence to enable it to develop.

List of Participants and Observers

Basil Bernstein, Institute of Education, University of London
Miss C. L. Boyle, Scottish Education Dept.
James Britton, Goldsmith's College, University of London
Dr. Gill Brown, Dept. of Linguistics, University of Edinburgh
Tom Brown, Moray House College of Education
J. S. Bruner, Dept of Expt. Psychology, University of Oxford
J. W. Casciani, Jordanhill College of Education
Dr. Margaret M. Clark, Dept. of Psychology, University of Strathclyde
Mrs. Ruth Clark, Dept. of Linguistics, University of Edinburgh
Dr. Marie Clay, Dept. of Education, University of Auckland, N.Z.
Clive Criper, Dept. of Linguistics, University of Edinburgh
Alan Davies, Dept. of Linguistics, University of Edinburgh
Mrs. Anne Dockrell, Queen Margaret College, Edinburgh
Bryan Dockrell, Scottish Council for Research in Education
Dr. Margaret Donaldson, Dept. of Psychology, University of Edinburgh
Miss K. Dougall, primary teacher, Edinburgh Corporation
Nelson Francis, Brown University
Mrs. N. Francis, Brown University
Colin Fraser, Dept. of Psychology, University of Bristol
W. Gatherer, Scottish Education Dept.
Patrick Griffiths, Dept. of Linguistics, University of Edinburgh
M. A. K. Halliday, Center for Advanced Study in the Behavioural Sciences, Stanford, Cal.
Mrs. Elisabeth Ingram, Dept. of Linguistics, University of Edinburgh
John Merritt, Education Faculty, Open University
A. Milne, Scottish Education Dept.
J. G. Morris, Scottish Education Dept.
Henry Nathan, University of Paris
J. D. Nisbet, Dept. of Education, Aberdeen University
Mrs. Arabella Pope, Educational Research Board, SSRC
John Powell, Scottish Council for Research in Education
Miss J. F. Reid, Dept. of Educational Sciences, University of Edinburgh
Mrs. E. Sestini, Education Dept., University of Leeds
John Sinclair, English Dept., University of Birmingham
A. Sloman, Dept. of Philosophy, University of Sussex
H. H. Speitel, Linguistic Survey, University of Edinburgh
Dr. Joan Tough, Education Dept., University of Leeds
H. G. Widdowson, Dept. of Linguistics, University of Edinburgh

(Affiliations are as of January 1973)